IMAGING PLACE

IMAGINING PLACE

Photographs

of a Tall Grass Prairie - Eastern Deciduous Forest Ecotome

by Carll Goodpasture

Imago ans Gjettum Norway

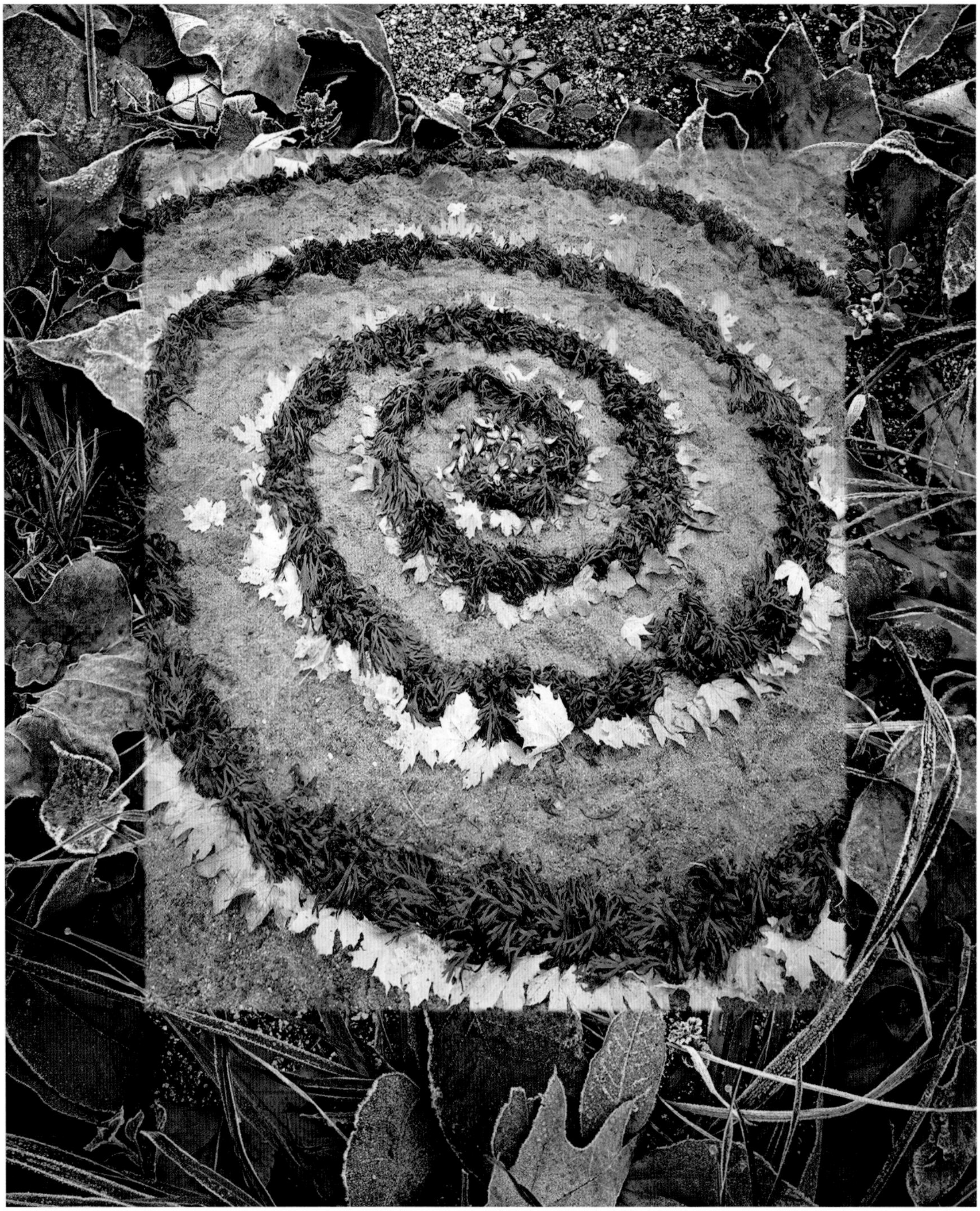

A place where Black Elk might have walked

Introductory Note

These photographs speak of place and of the emergent property of interconnectedness that sustains life on the Earth. The intention is an homage to the first people to inhabit the land with teaching and tradition in reverential recognition of their environment, the planet itself, as a living animate being. My camera work suggests that we listen to the roots of our ancient solidarity, and get on with the work of relearning nature consciousness in this fragile life space.

Preface

In the beginning, earth was space without form,
then through inhabitance places were created.

– Lawrence Buell, *The Future of Environmental Criticism*, 2005

Of all the concerns, both spiritual and physical, facing the world today, the most basic, in my view, is that of the interdependency between human beings and the earth. In the last century or two, an ideology of unrestrained industrial progress has displaced a vision of a human-earth relationship, with consequences that represent something utterly new on the planet: a level and a magnitude of materiality, and a pace of change hitherto unknown to human consciousness.

As Thomas Berry has pointed out, the twentieth century eliminated the terror of the unknown darkness of nature by devastating nature itself. But he, among others, perceives a change in the wind, a hint that an evolution may be taking place in society such that once more we may be able to experience the immediacy of life, a change pointing to a renewal of earth process and a return to the primordial community of the universe, the earth, and all living things.

How this might come about, nobody knows, but I find it interesting to note that the spiritual philosophy implicit in Native American visionary experience mirrors, in its expression, the evolutionary conclusion that all life forms are related, the ecological tenet that all things are connected, and the Gaia hypothesis that the earth is a living, self-regulating system.

Enchanted visions, be they ancient or modern, are in conflict with the technological world. As would be expected from the dominant ideology at present, new strains of psychic energy have been let loose on the planet and have largely taken over control of the physical functioning of earth's biological systems. The spiritual history of the human community can be seen to have followed an evolutionary process culminating, in post-modern times, in a unique human predicament.

Although wilderness has largely vanished, and what little remains will never again be without human influence, the human genome survives and flourishes, though still completely dependent on the healthy functioning of natural ecosystems. From my observations of the current human predicament, it seems that the very structure of human consciousness is in peril.

What provides the human mind-brain system with an integrating and unifying source of dream and myth material is our ecology and our natural history. They provide us with the perceptual experience of ourselves as a part of the natural world. It would seem that to ignore our mammalian nature and evolutionary heritage threatens not only wilderness on the planet, but the very nature of human consciousness as well.

The Photography

This is a story about a place where I once lived. While the landscape has been transformed from wilderness to modernity, something of its native spirit nevertheless seems to live on in the land. I have tried to use my camera as an imagining tool to envision a sense of the sacred in the land.

The photographs present a view of remnants and reminders of a tall grass prairie – eastern deciduous forest ecotome that today is a fertile and prosperous industrial ecosystem. In this region of the United States, where Minnesota meets North Dakota, extensive agricultural development and urbanization have left none of the prairie and forest biome undisturbed; indeed, only a small fraction is still intact. Yet in places such as Buffalo River, Maplewood, and Itasca State Parks, scattered patches of natural habitat survive.

These are the ancestral lands of the American Plains Indian nations, a group of people whose culture and biology were directly dependent on the ecosystem services in their environment. As pre-European caretakers of the land they lived on, they believed that all things had an animate nature, as if alive; and were thus aware of the material and spiritual needs of their environment in its totality. The profound insight that we are not isolated beings but are connected to all things was eloquently expressed long before the turn of the last century by Native American visionaries. One of these speakers was Black Elk, an Oglala Sioux traditional lore-keeper and ritualist who, since he was born in 1862, had known at first hand the old ways of indigenous life on the Great Plains.

As an artist, I am inspired by the spiritual beliefs of these first people, who through their traditional wisdom once maintained their environment in harmony with its natural character.

As a biologist and an ecologist, I am aware that the natural conditions in which we live constrain our cultural expression. To find and then photograph places that embodied my mental images and would thus enable me to express an ecocentric imagination, I searched the landscape like a lost child seeking the comfort of an elder generation; I read the history of the indigenous people; and I sought out places where, from the look and feel of them, it seemed that Black Elk might have walked. In a poetic sense, my eye has been listening for ancient voices in the land. In a conceptual sense, the camera work is an attempt to visualize the elements of human consciousness that contribute to our understanding of the natural and cultural history of a place.

The Photographs

The Story

1 A way of birch in the moon of red cherries
2 Winter solstice sun appearing in the moon of popping trees
3 Tree family along Buffalo River in the moon of frost in the tepee
4 Cottonwoods crossing Buffalo River in the moon of falling leaves
5 Oak tree branching in the moon of popping trees
6 Seven grandfathers mourning in the moon of red cherries

Vision

7 Headwaters of the Mississippi in the moon of frost in the tepee
8 Dragonfly sleeping place in the moon of the changing seasons
9 Wooly mullein in a frosty meadow when the calves grow hair
10 Forest floor leavings in the moon of red cherries
11 Buffalo River spirit in the moon of falling leaves
12 First place to snow along Buffalo River in the moon of falling leaves

Spirit Beings

13 Feather clouds over Maplewood in the moon of the changing seasons
14 Reflecting tree on Buffalo River in the moon of red cherries
15 Grandfather's spirit in Lake Itasca in the moon of the snowbird
16 Falling water in the moon of falling leaves
17 Dancing shore at Lake Lida in the moon of the changing seasons
18 Hole in Red River at Fargo in the moon of frost in the tepee

It was a wide land, wider than many looks could reach across, and yet I saw it all together, and what was far away was near too, because of the clear light that lived everywhere.

– Eagle Voice [1]

THE STORY

It is the story of all life that is holy and is good,
and of us two-leggeds sharing in it with the four-leggeds
and the wings of the air and all green things;
for these are children of one mother, and their father is one spirit.

Is not the sky a father and the earth a mother,
and are not all living things with feet or wings or roots their children?

The earth from whence we come
and at whose breast we suck as babes all our lives,
along with the animals and birds and grasses.

It means all these things and more than any man can understand.

This they tell: and if you think about it you can see that it is true. [2]

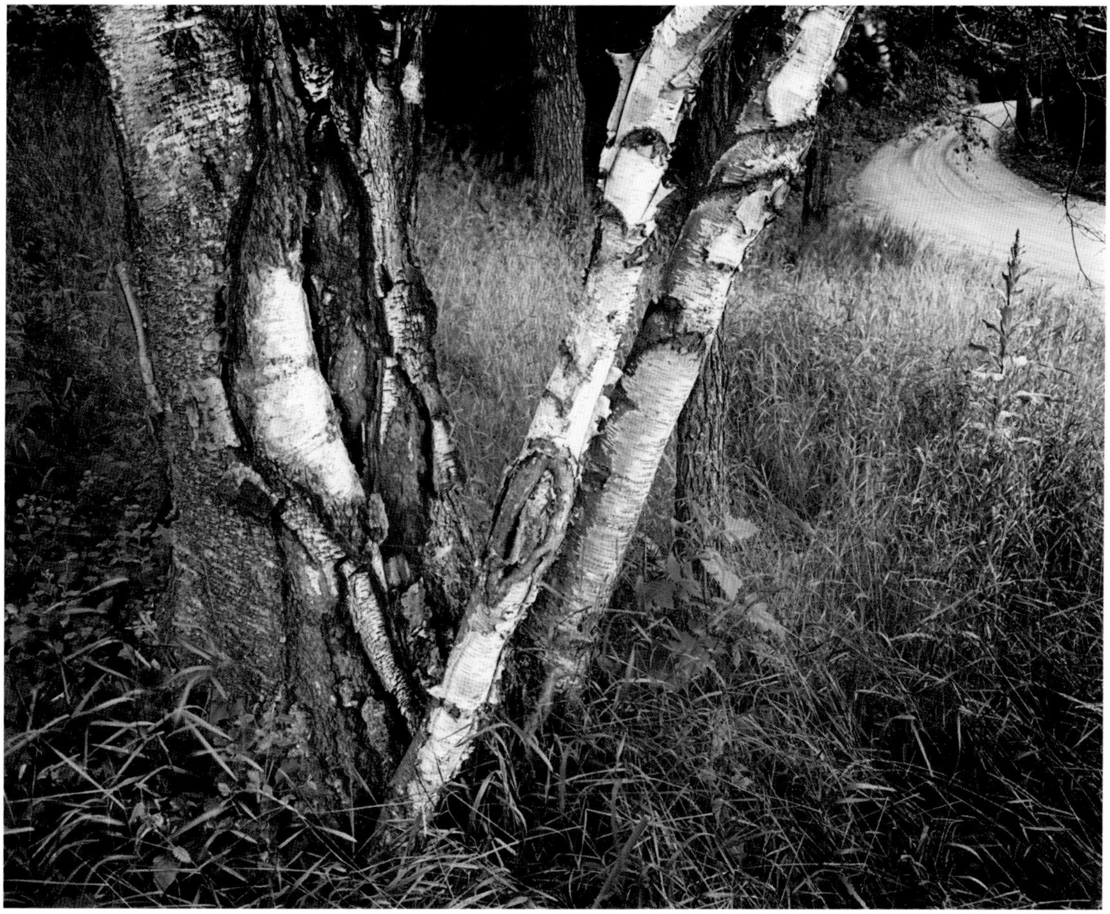

1. A way of birch

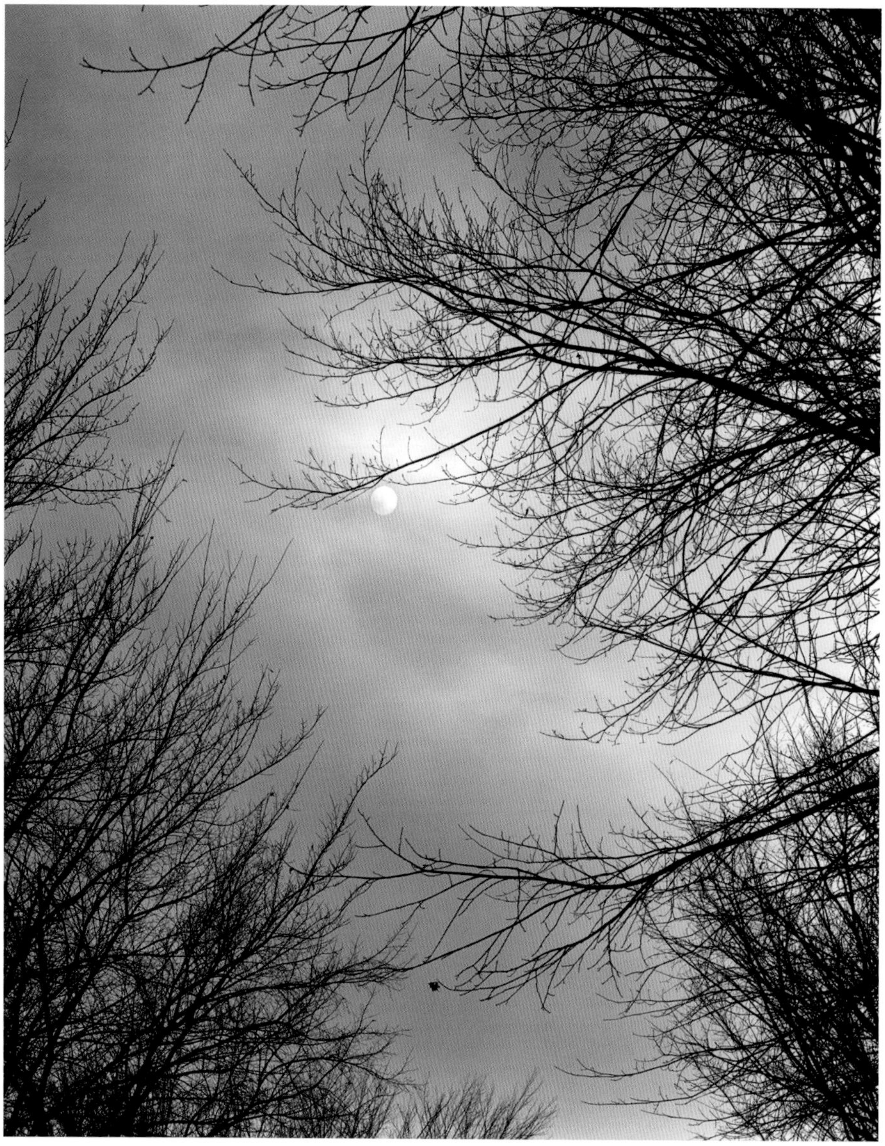

2. Winter solstice sun appearing

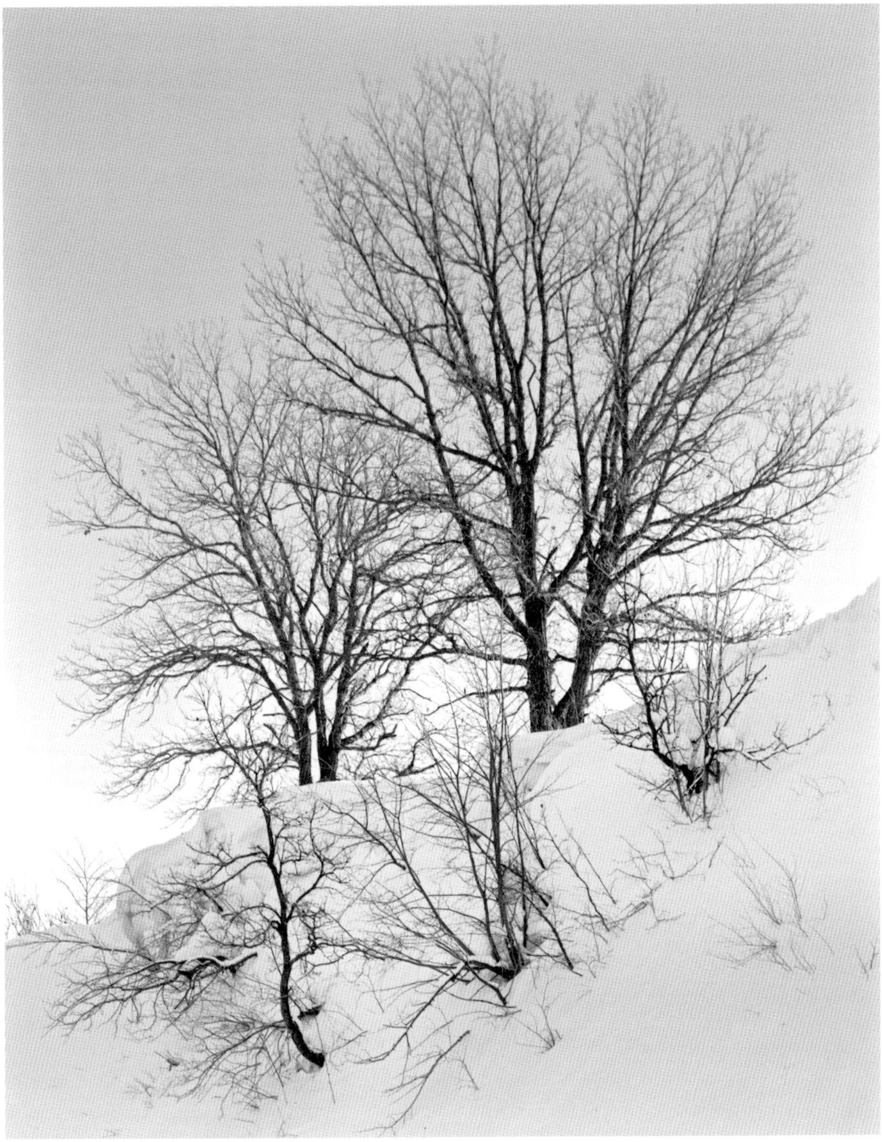

3. Tree family along Buffalo River

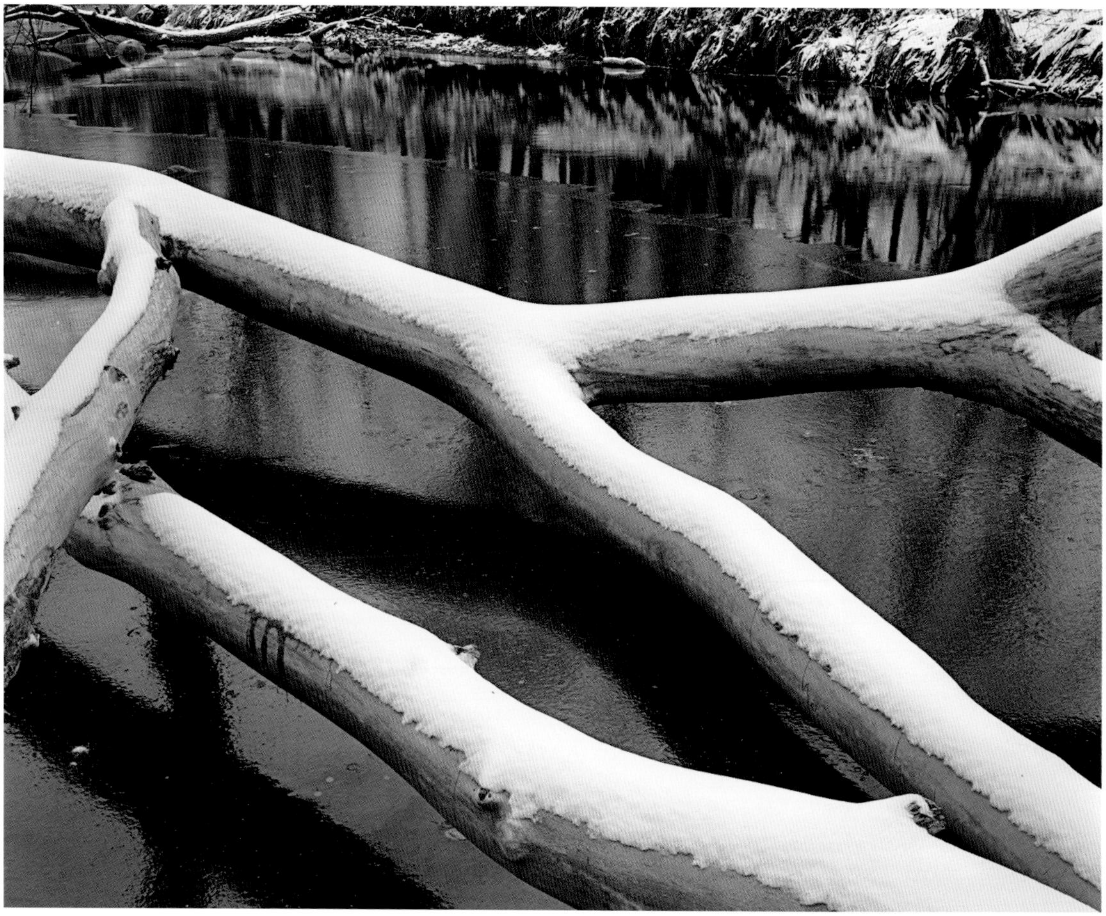

4. Cottonwoods crossing Buffalo River

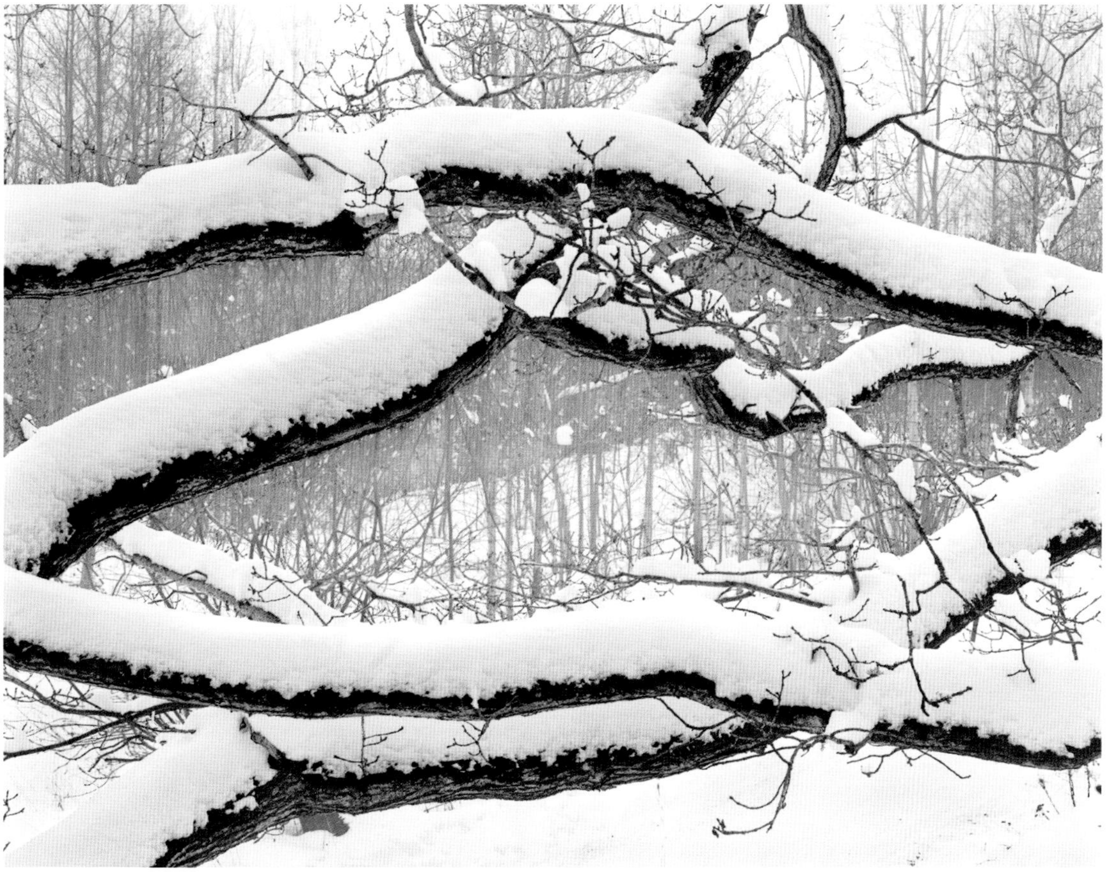

5. Oak tree branching

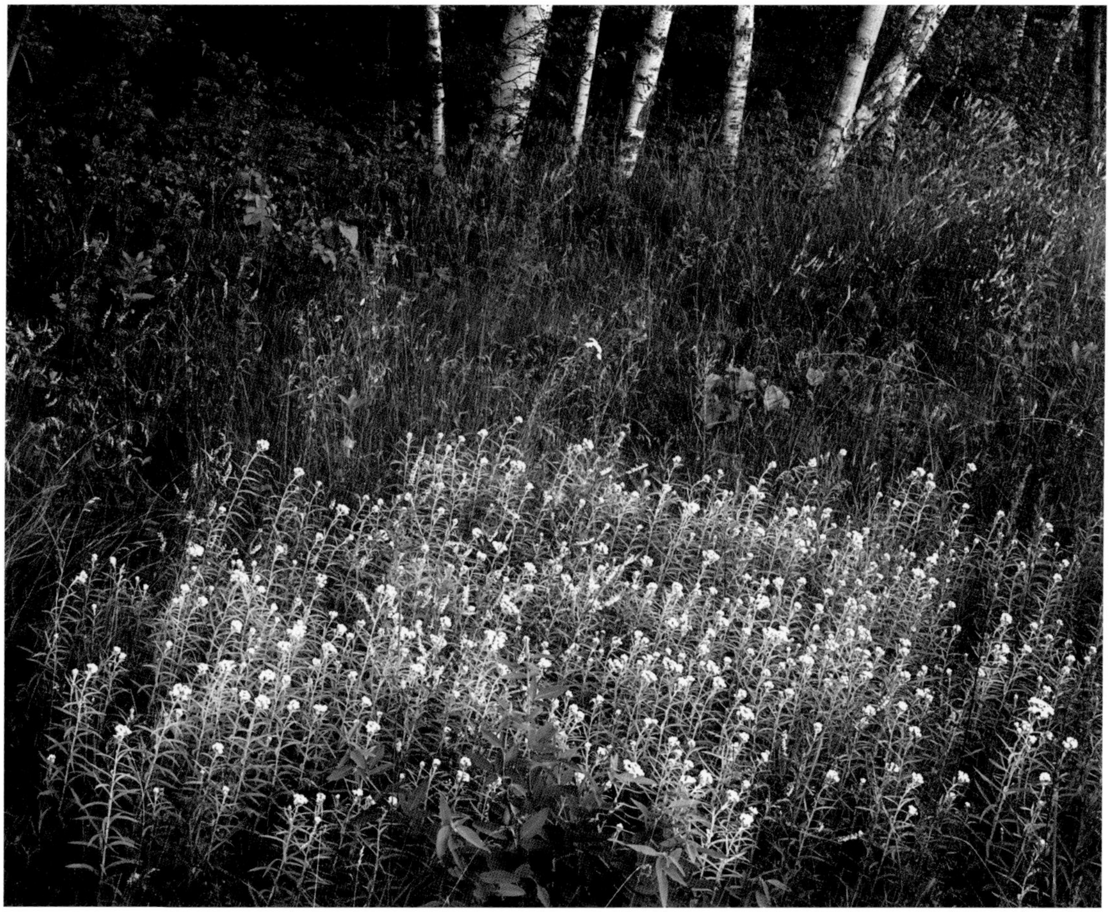

6. Seven grandfather's mourning

Vision

Crazy Horse dreamed and went into the world
where there is nothing but the spirits of all things.

That is the real world behind this one and everything we see
and everything we hear is something like a shadow from that world.

The trees and the grass and the stones and everything were made of spirit.

Nothing was hard and everything seemed to float.

It was this vision that gave him his great power.
He had only to think of that world to be in it again. [3]

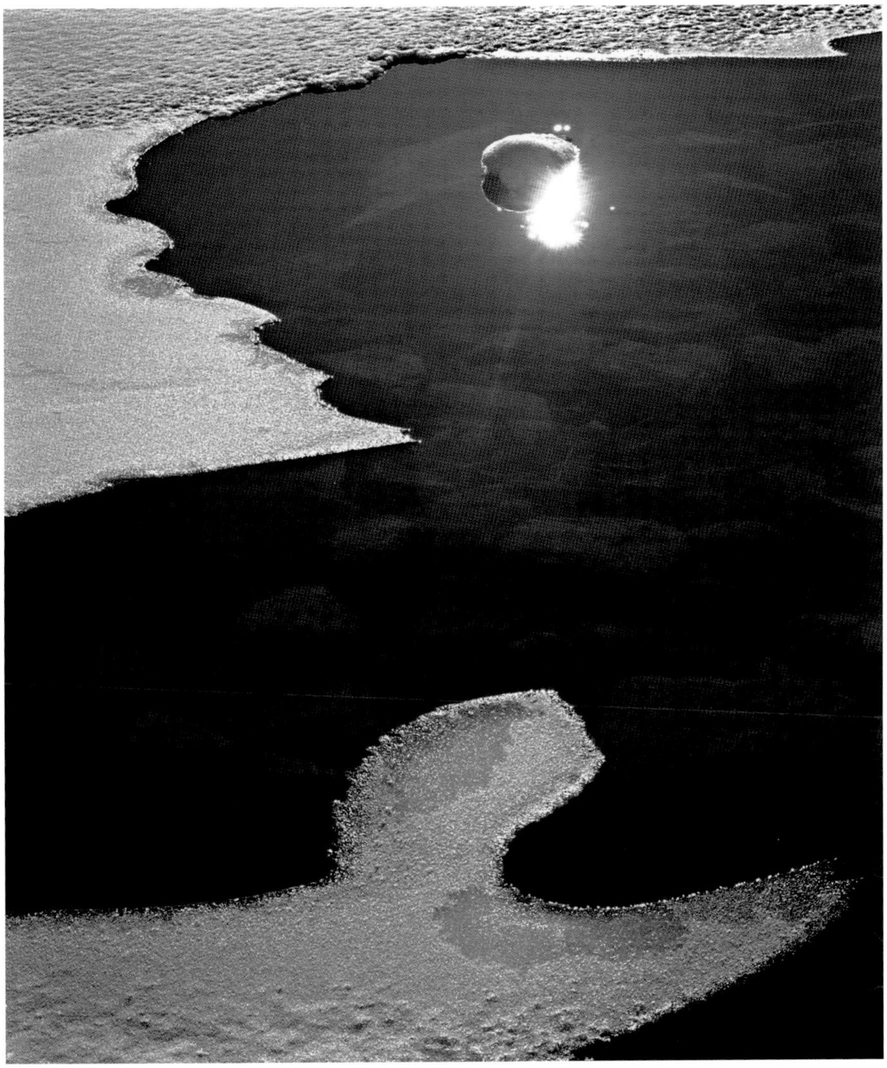

7. Headwaters of the Mississippi

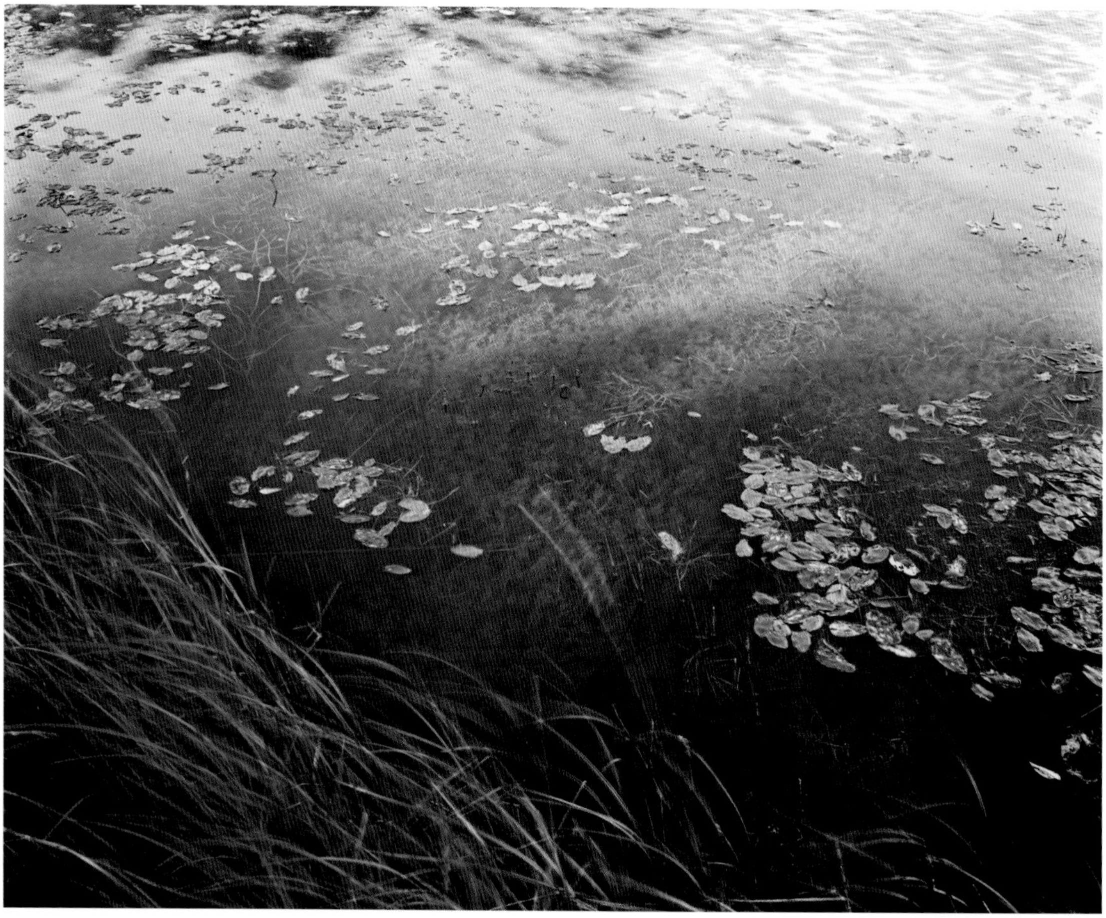

8. Dragonfly sleeping place

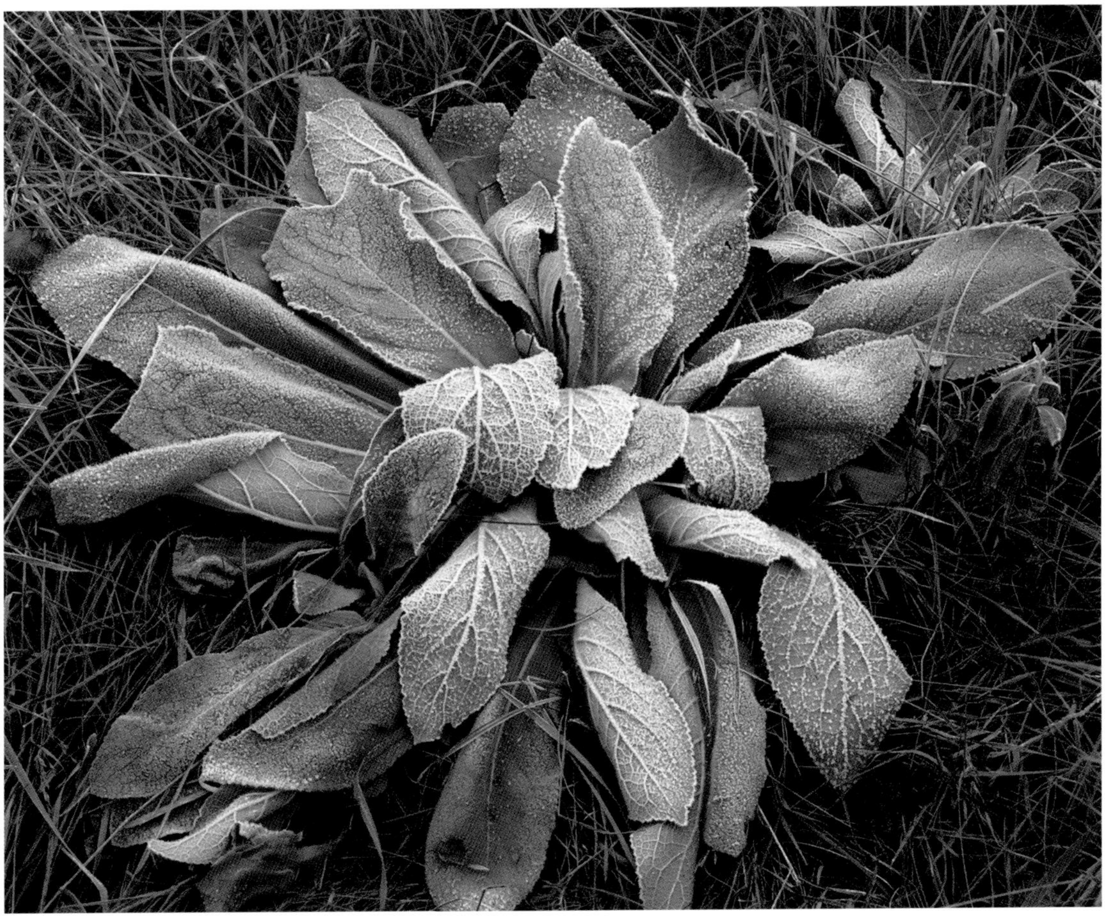

9. Woolly mullein in a frosty Maplewood meadow

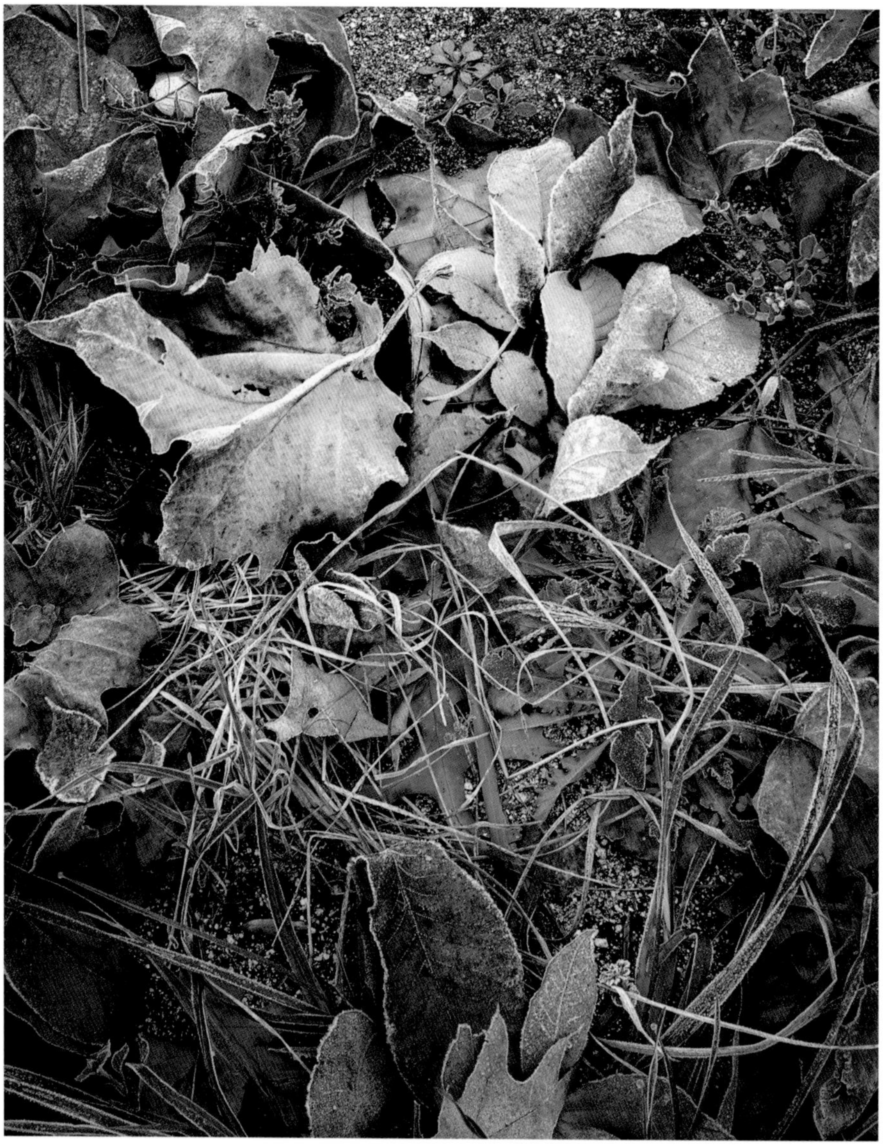

10. Forest floor leavings

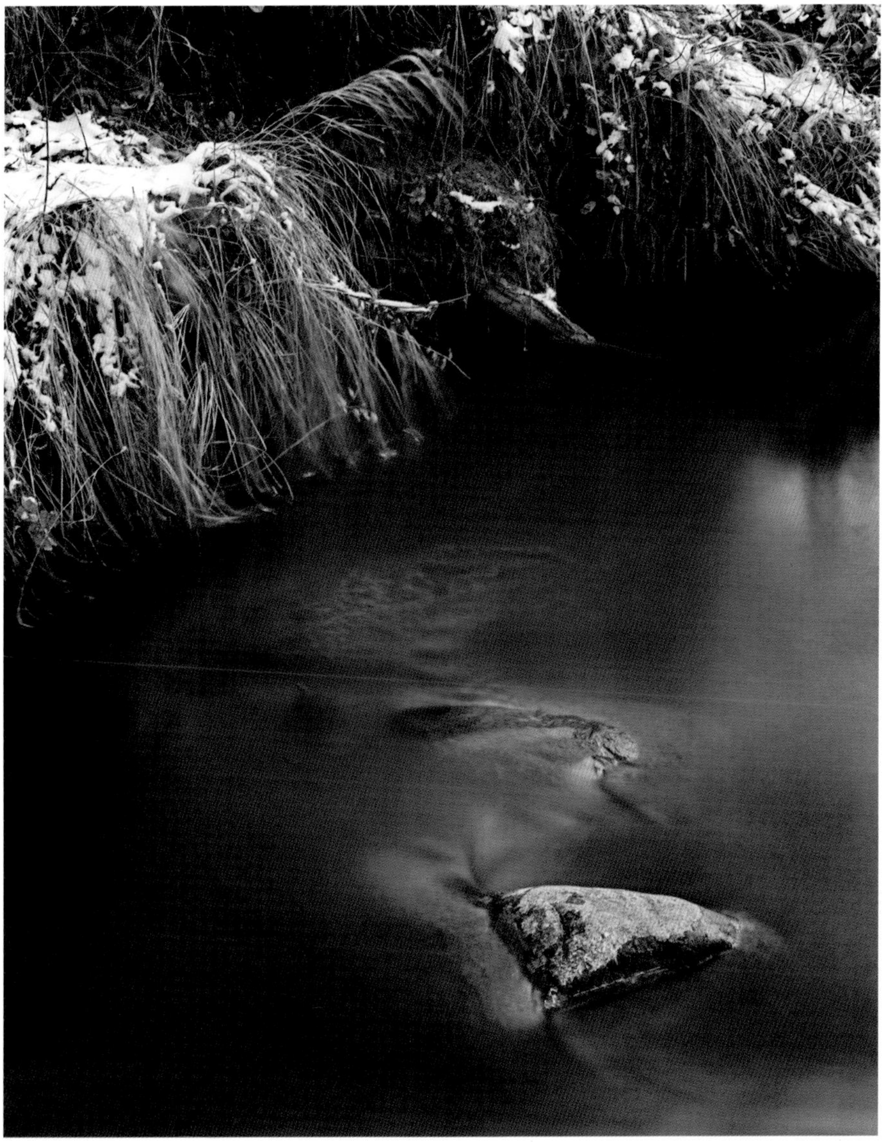

11. Buffalo River spirit

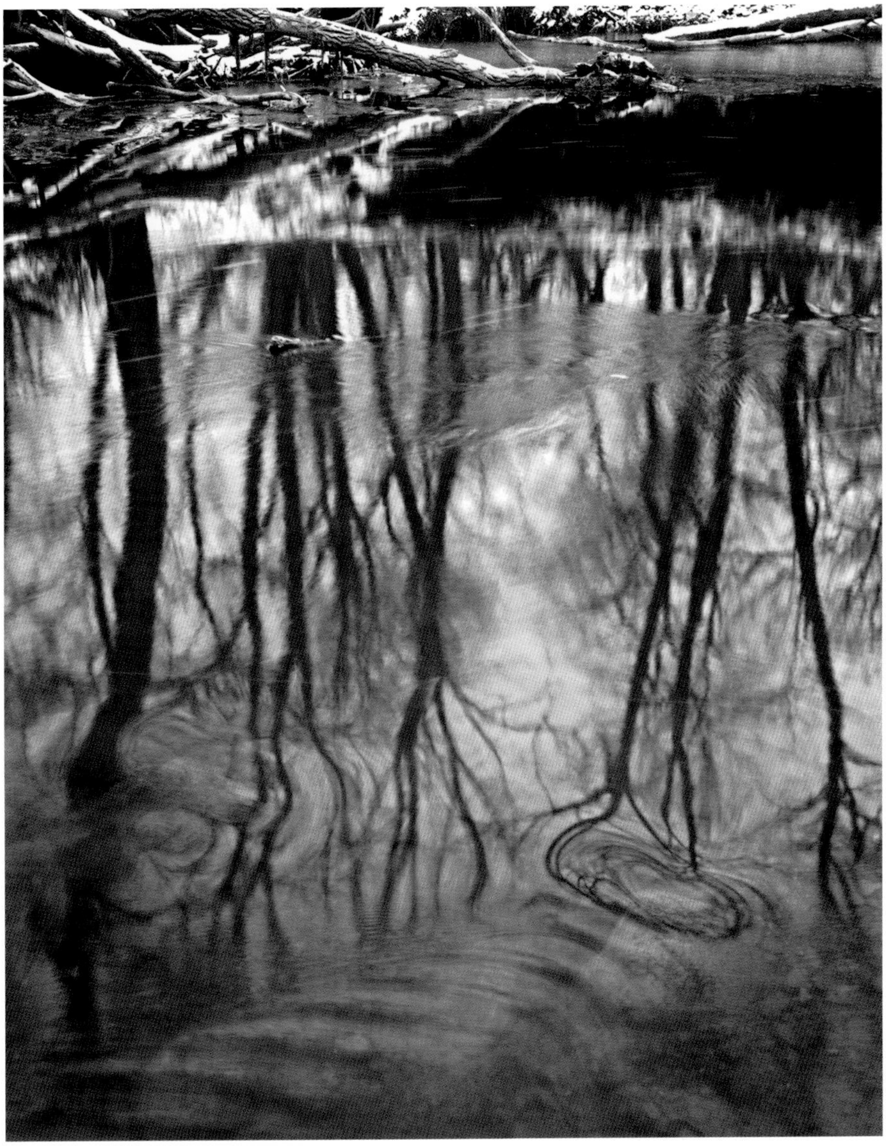

12. First place to snow along Buffalo River

Spirit Beings

I was seeing in the sacred manner the shapes of all things in the spirit, and the shape of all the things as they must live together as one being.

His voice was not loud, but it went all over the universe and filled it. There was nothing that did not hear, and it was more beautiful than anything can be. It was so beautiful that nothing anywhere could keep from dancing.

The beings danced, and all the circled horses. The leaves on the trees, the grasses on the hills and in the valleys, the waters in the creeks and in the rivers and the lakes, the four-legged and the two-legged and the wings of the air –

all danced together to the music of the stallion's song. [4]

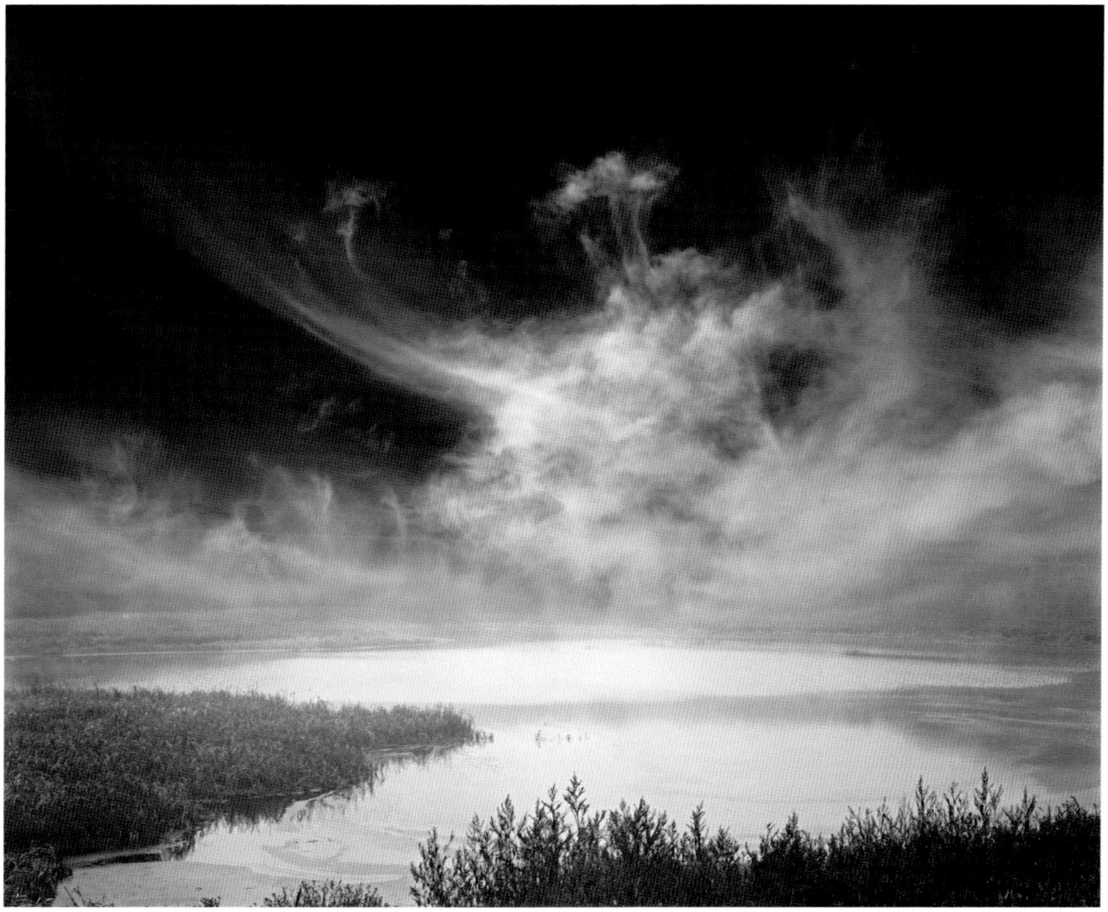

13. Feather clouds over Maplewood

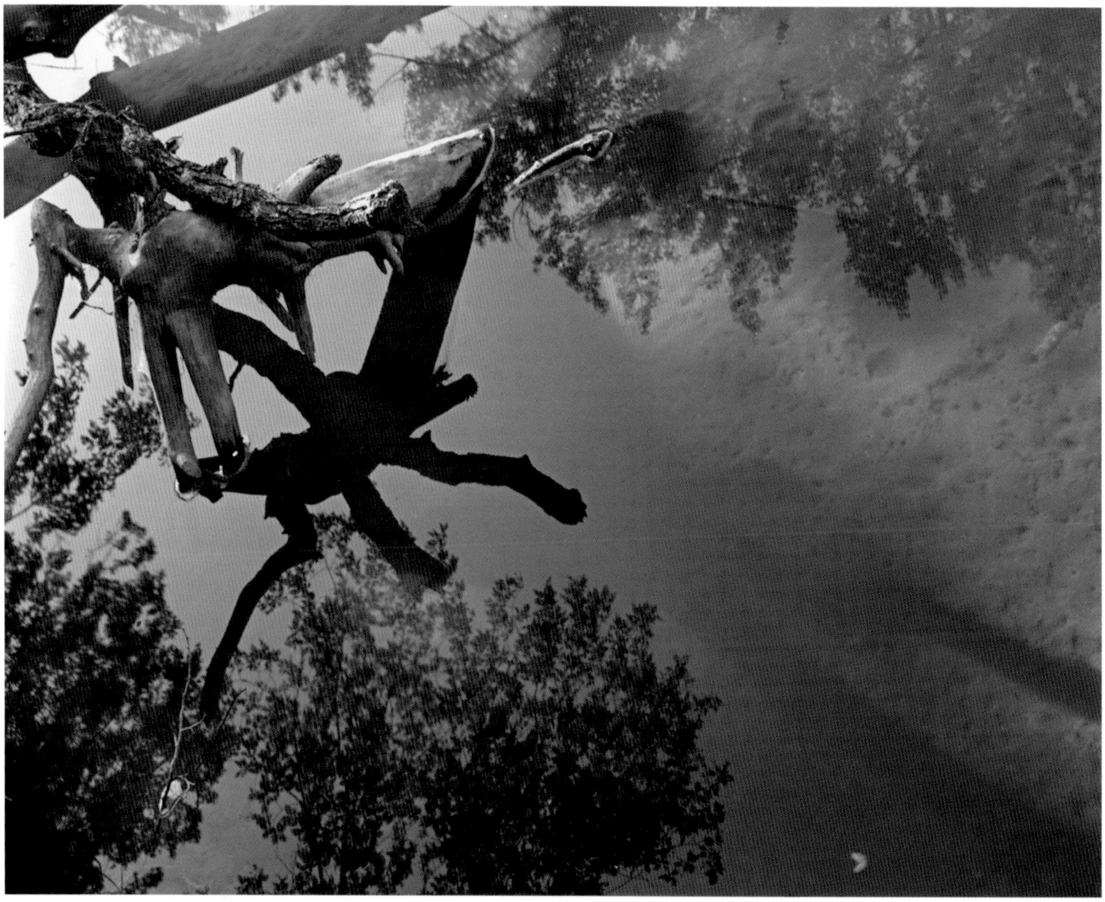

14. Tree reflecting on Buffalo River

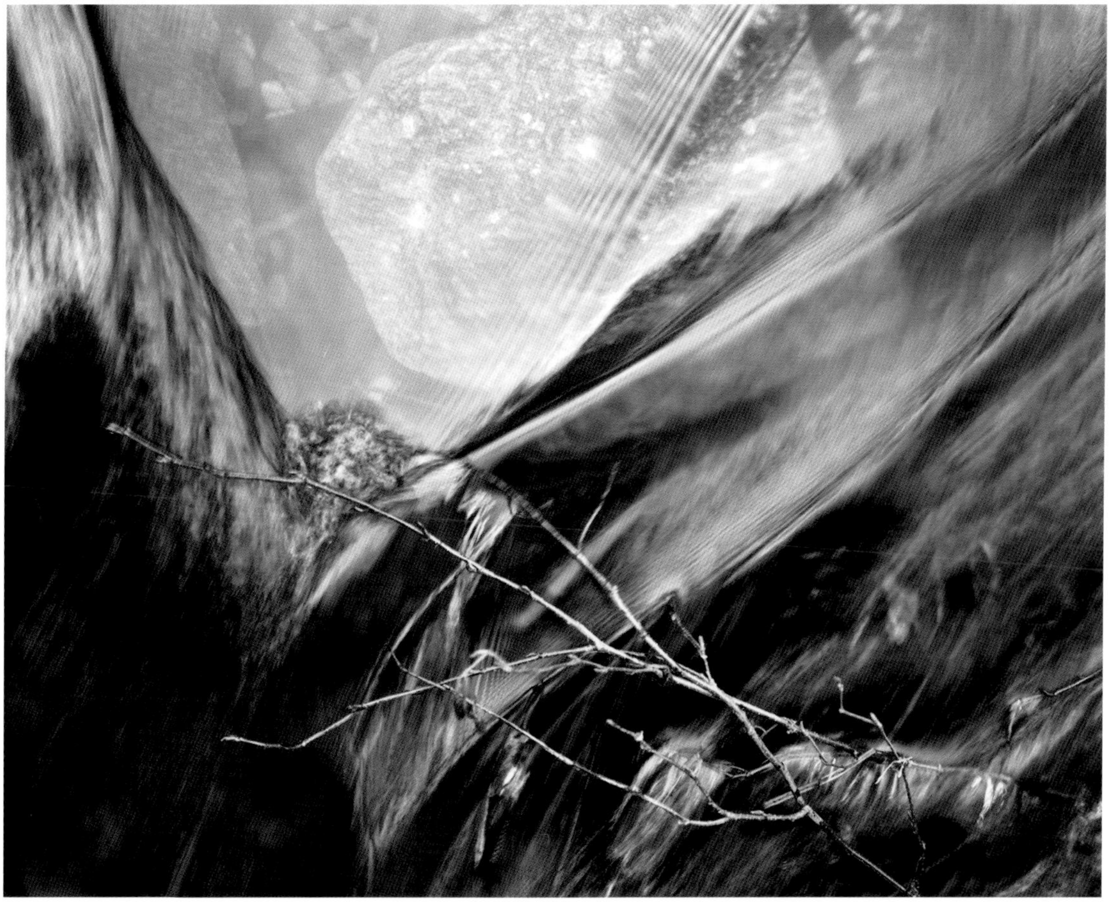

15. Grandfather's spirit in Lake Itasca

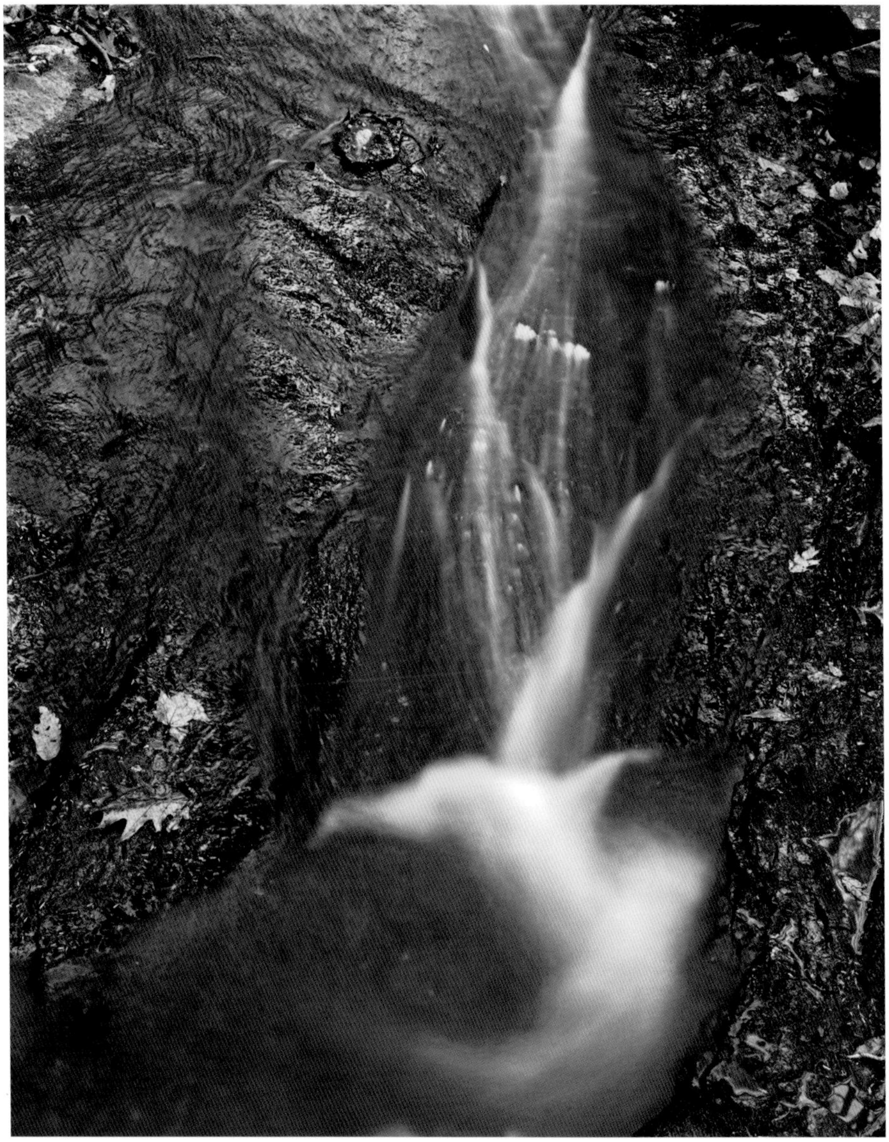

16. Falling water

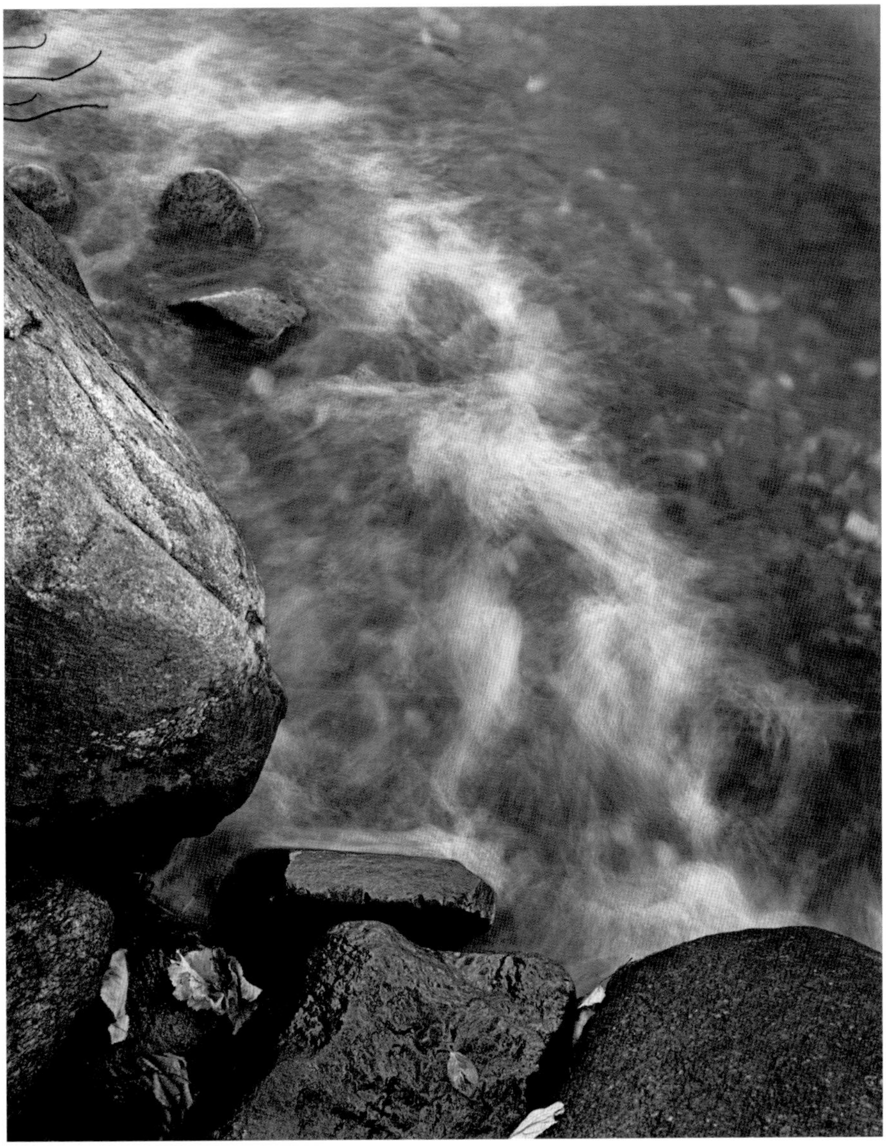

17. Dancing shore at Lake Lida

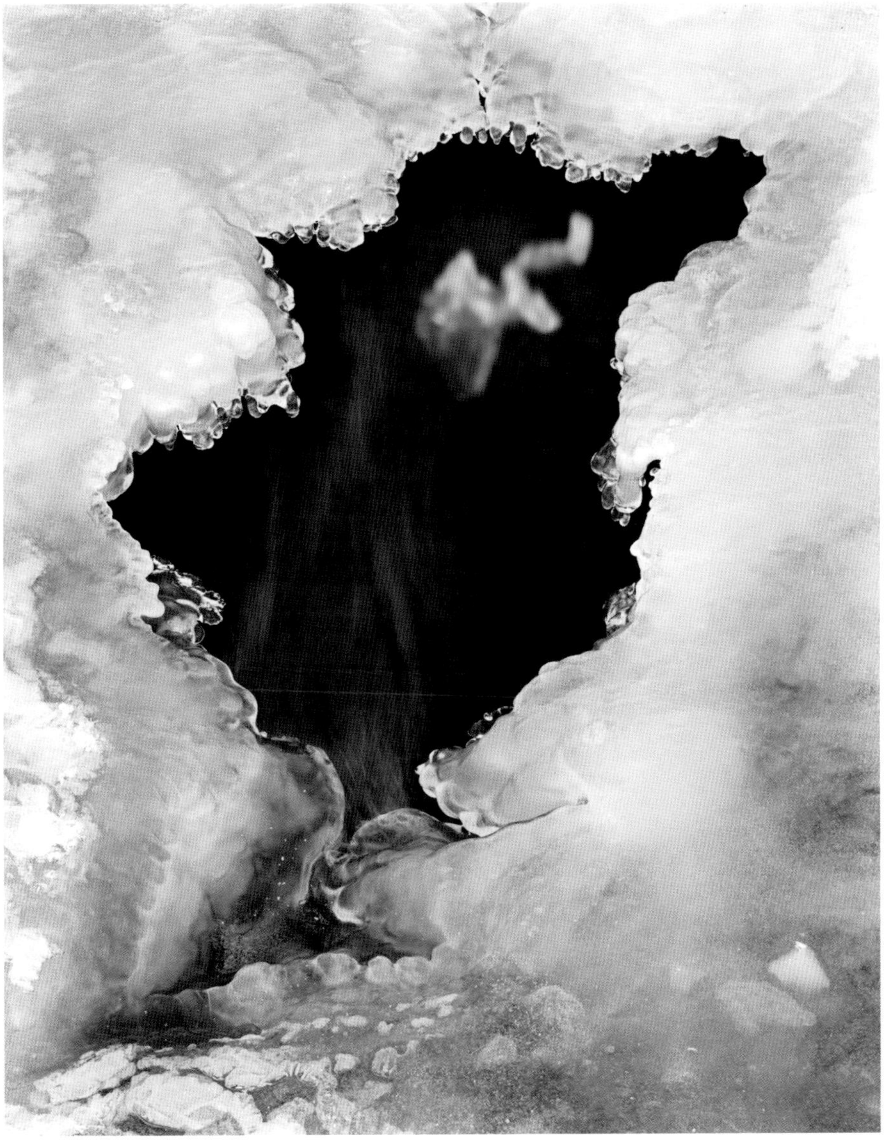

18. Hole in Red River at Fargo

The Great Mystery

Wakan Tanka, you have existed from the first

Thunder-beings, you have existed from the first

Wing Flappers, who existed first

Spotted Eagle, most powerful

Sunrise, no other creature may be mentioned

South, no other creature may be mentioned

Great Mystery, you were the first to exist,
this earth you created and placed here

Behold this day, for it is yours to make.

Now you shall stand upon the center of the earth to see.

And I saw that it was holy. [5]

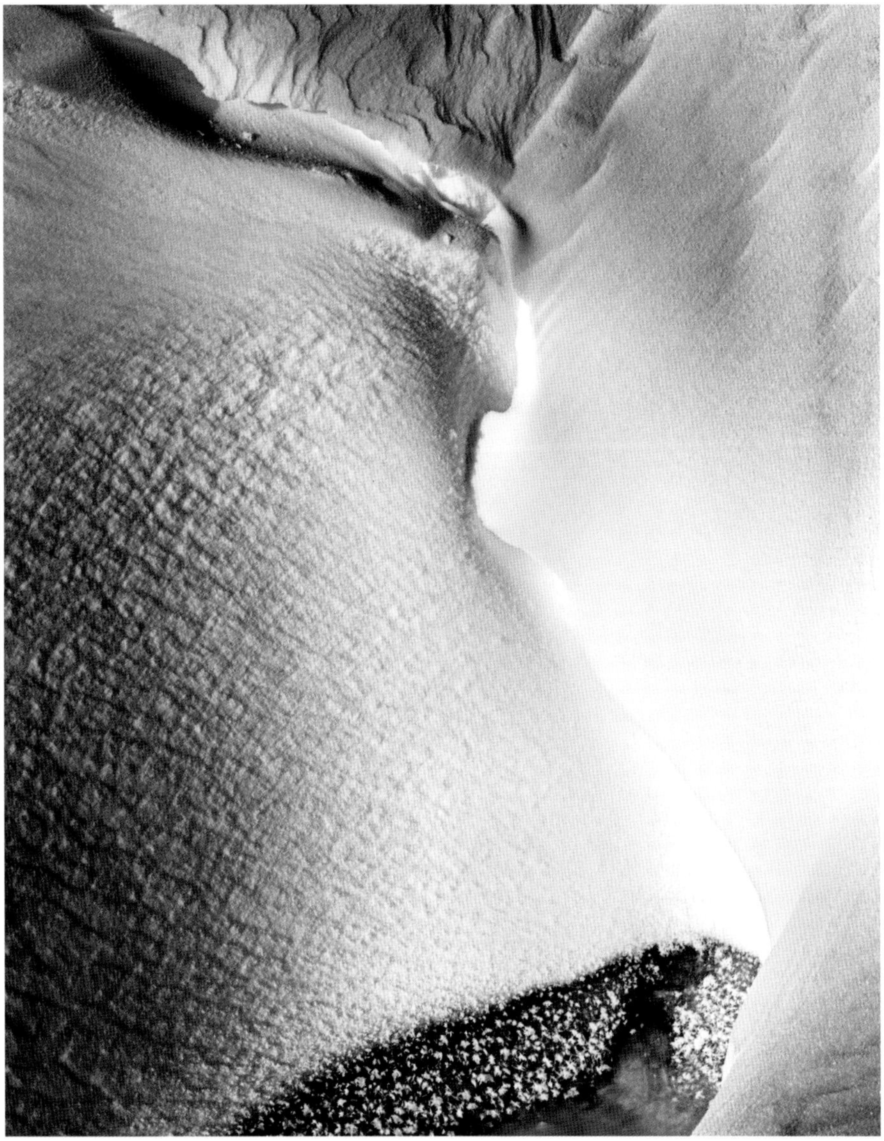

19. Moon light on snow drifting

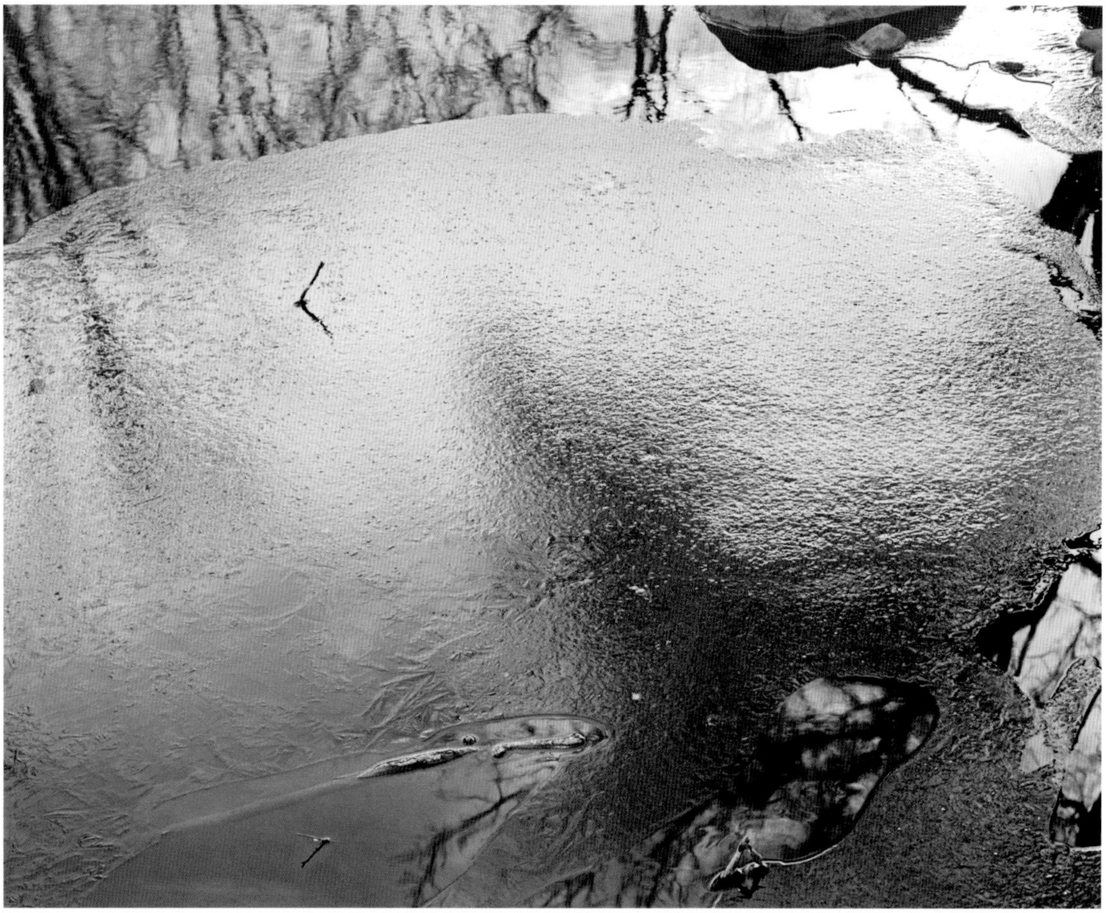

20. Ice forming on Buffalo River

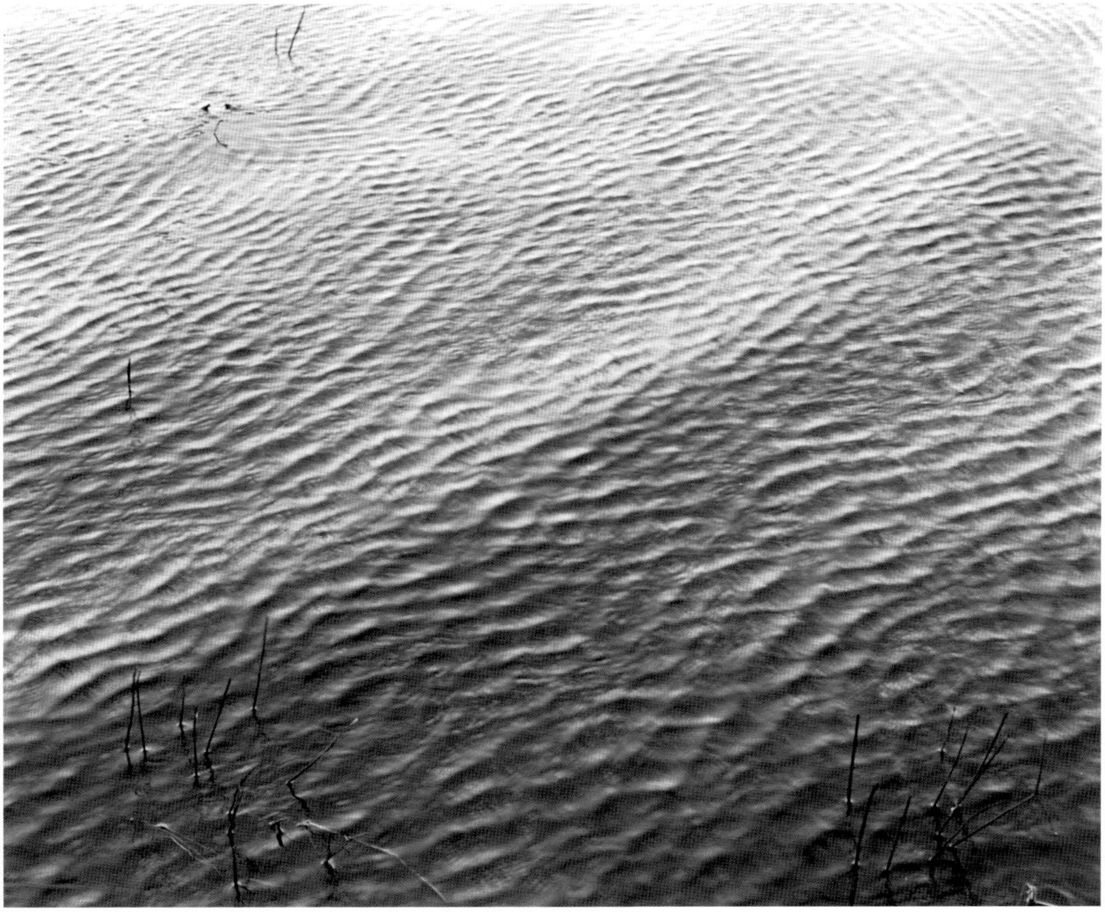

21. Wind rolling over Bass Lake

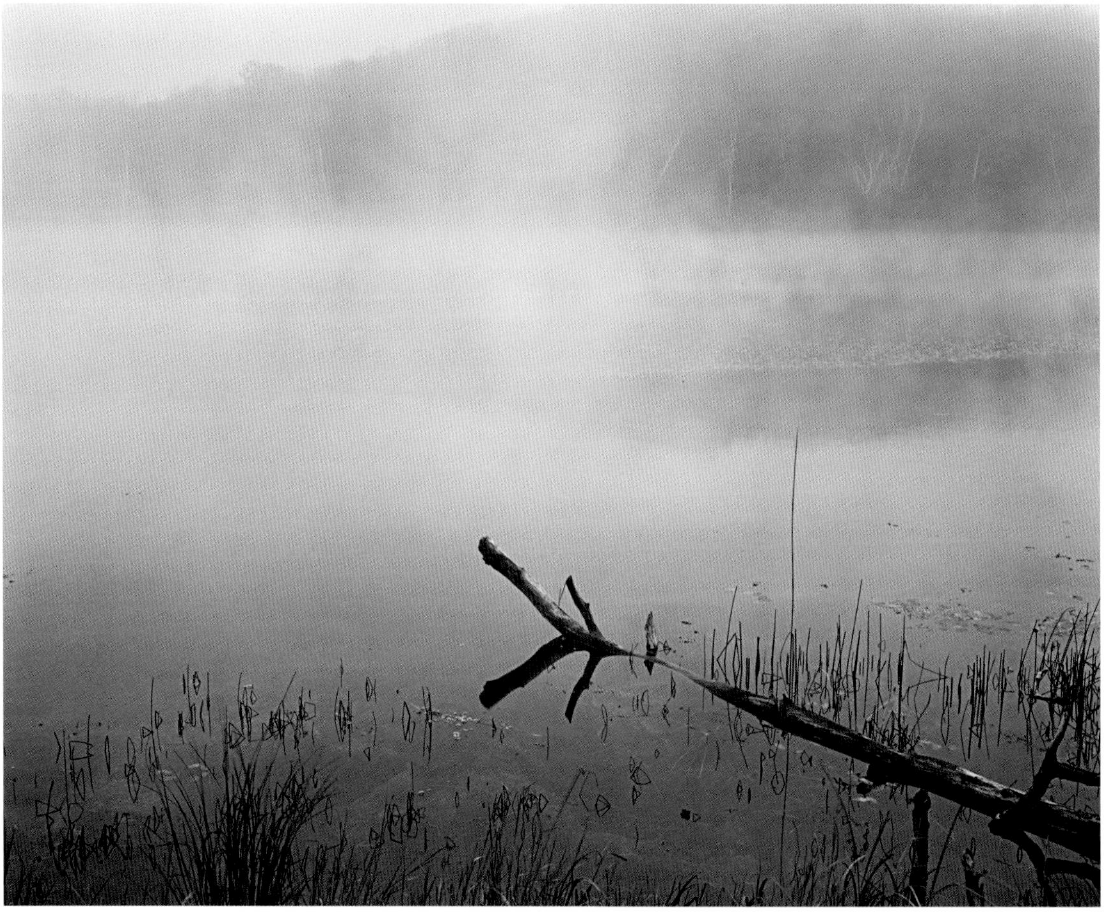

22. Morning fog rising at Maplewood

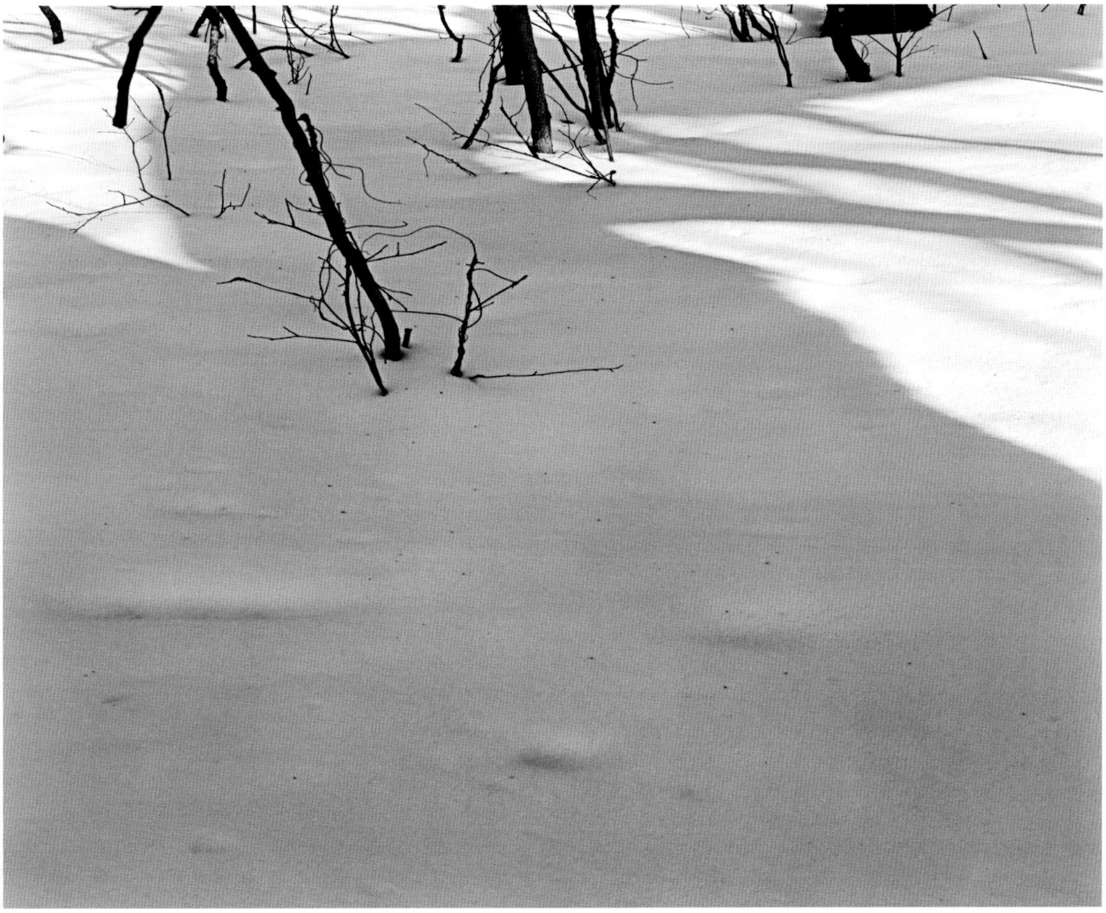

23. Snow shadows in Moorhead

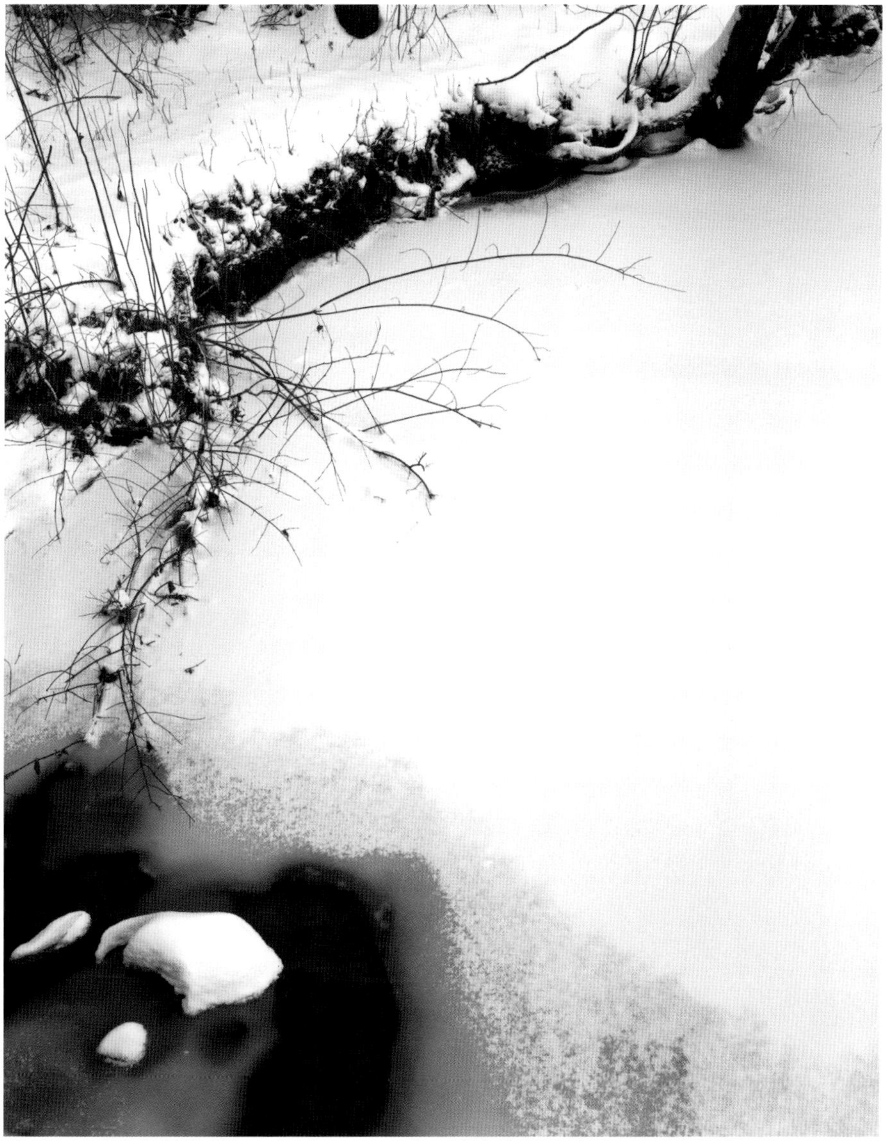

24. Little creek resting

Oneness

All the powers of the world
the heavens and the star peoples
and the red and the blue sacred days
and all things that move in the universe
in the rivers
the brooks
the springs
all waters
all trees that stand
all grasses of our Grandmother
all the sacred peoples of the universe [6]

Listen!
Realize our oneness with all things
know that all things are our relatives [7]

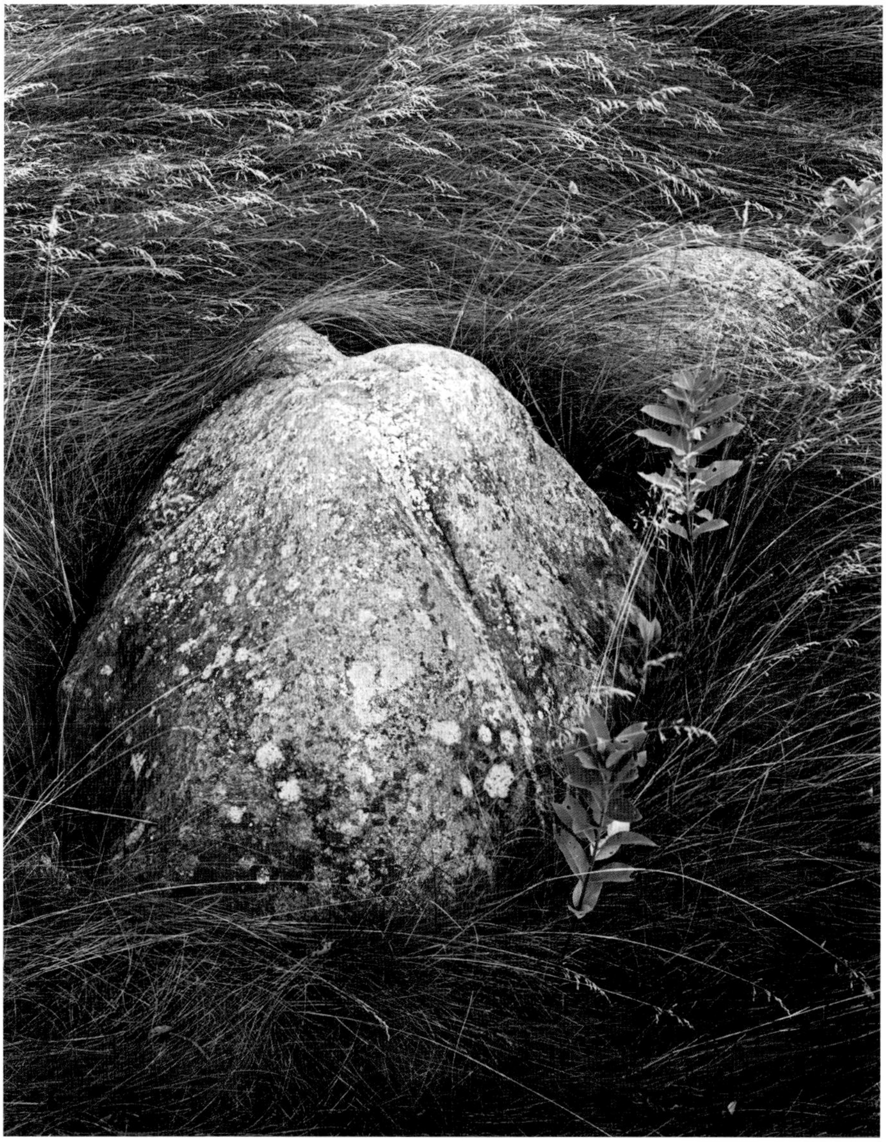

25. Prairie stones waiting

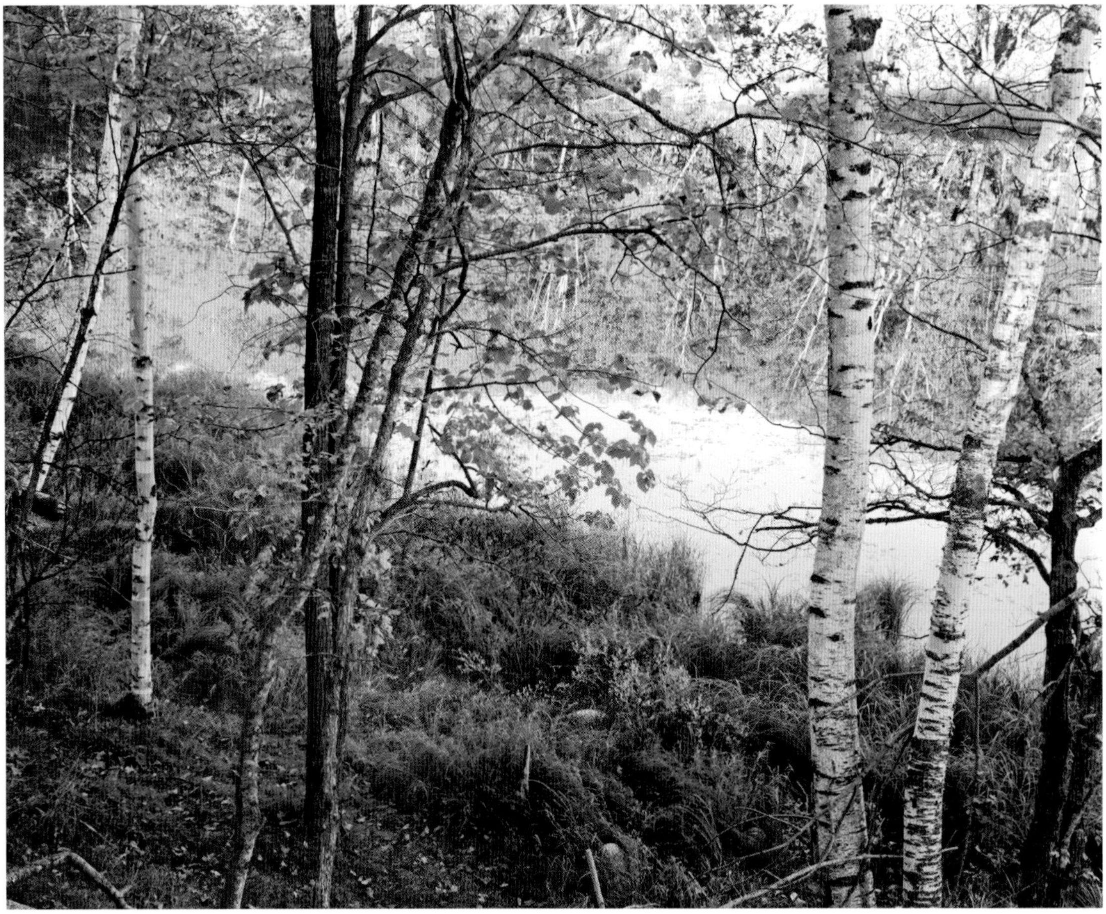

26. Path along Beers Lake

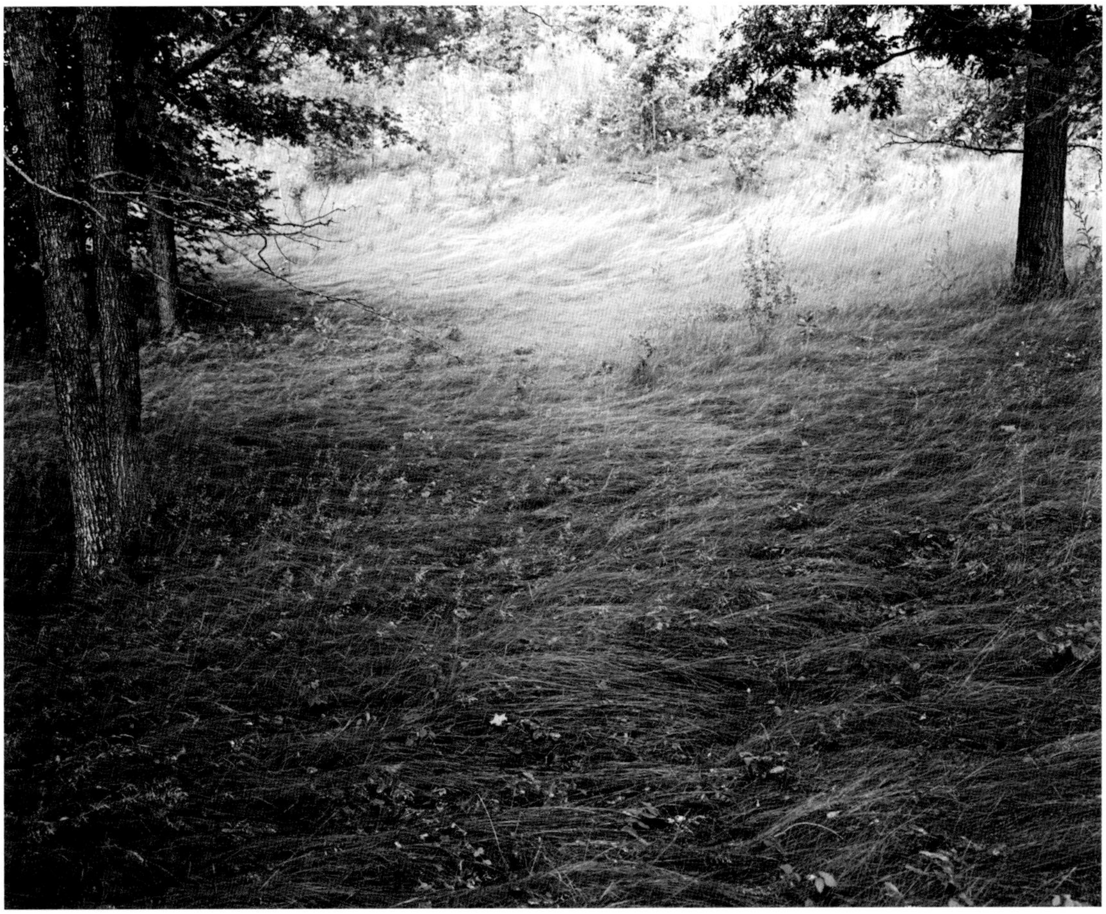

27. Fallen leaf

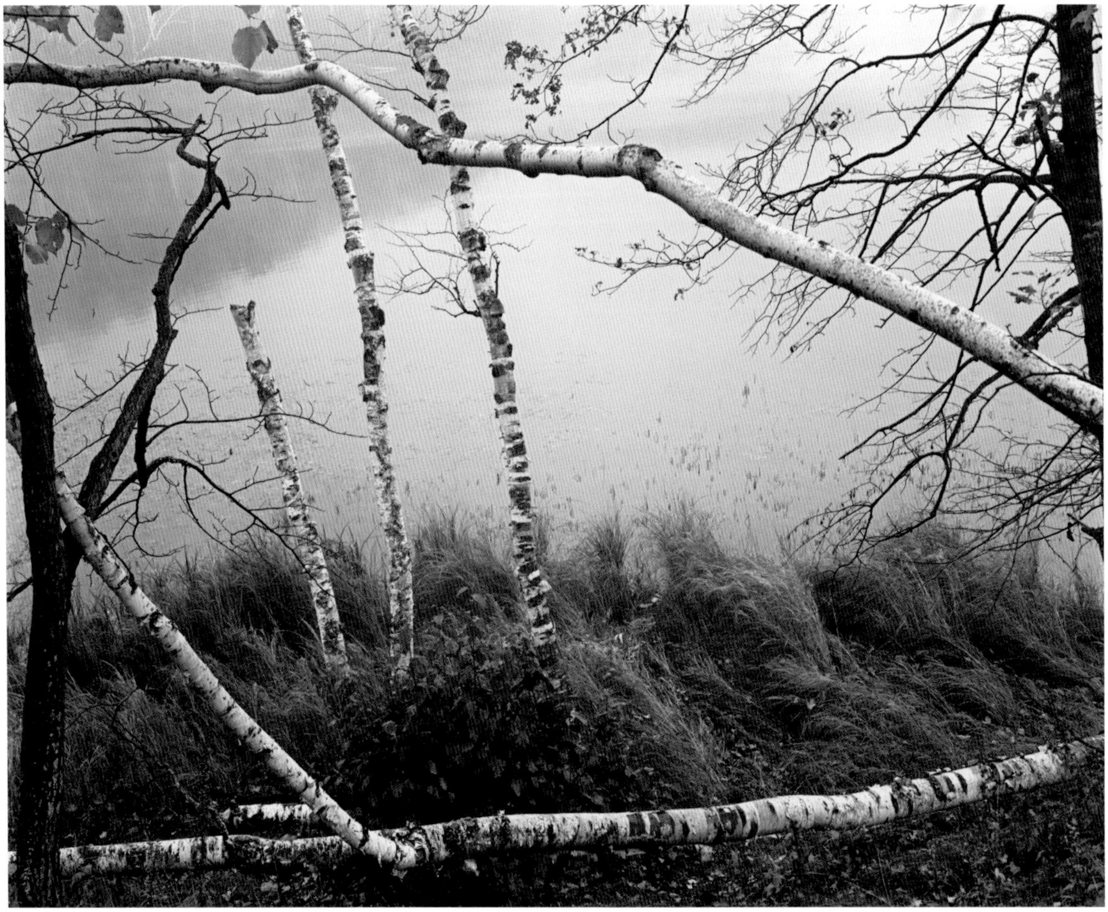

28. Sleeping birch

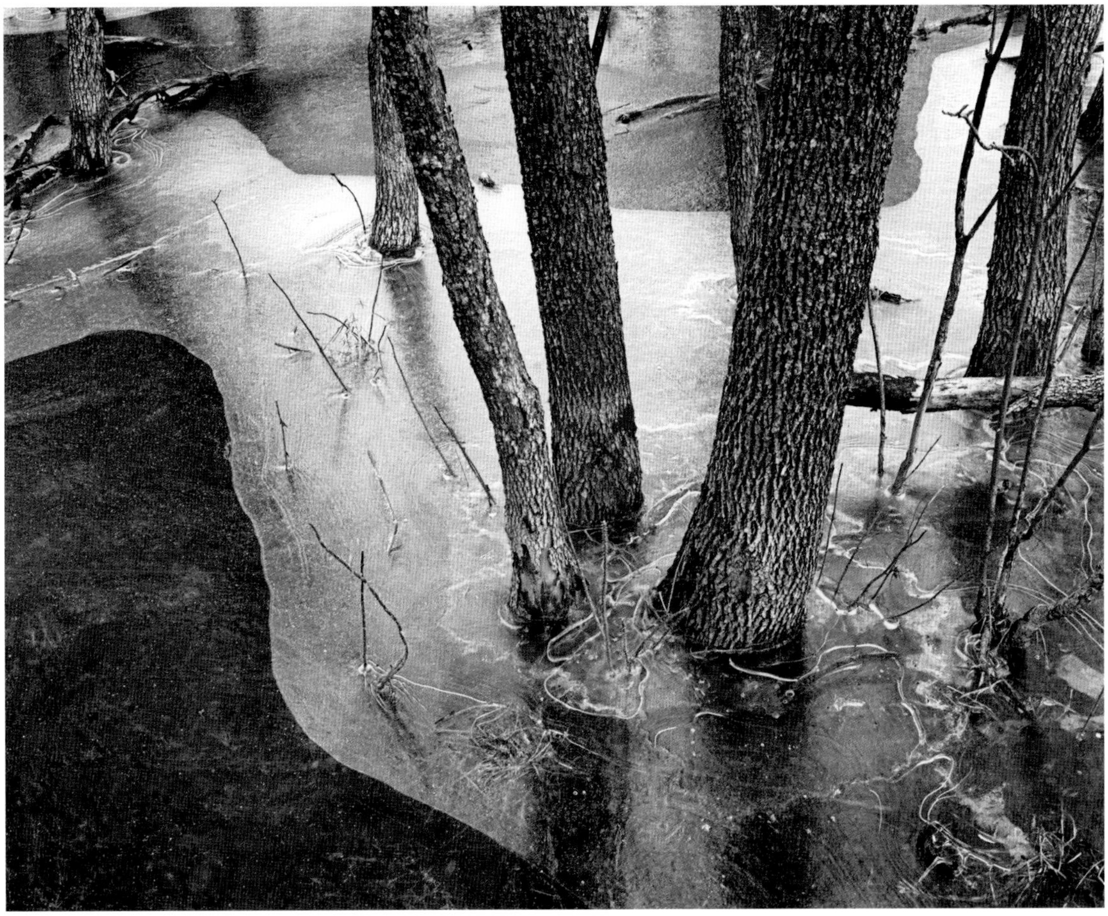

29. American elms

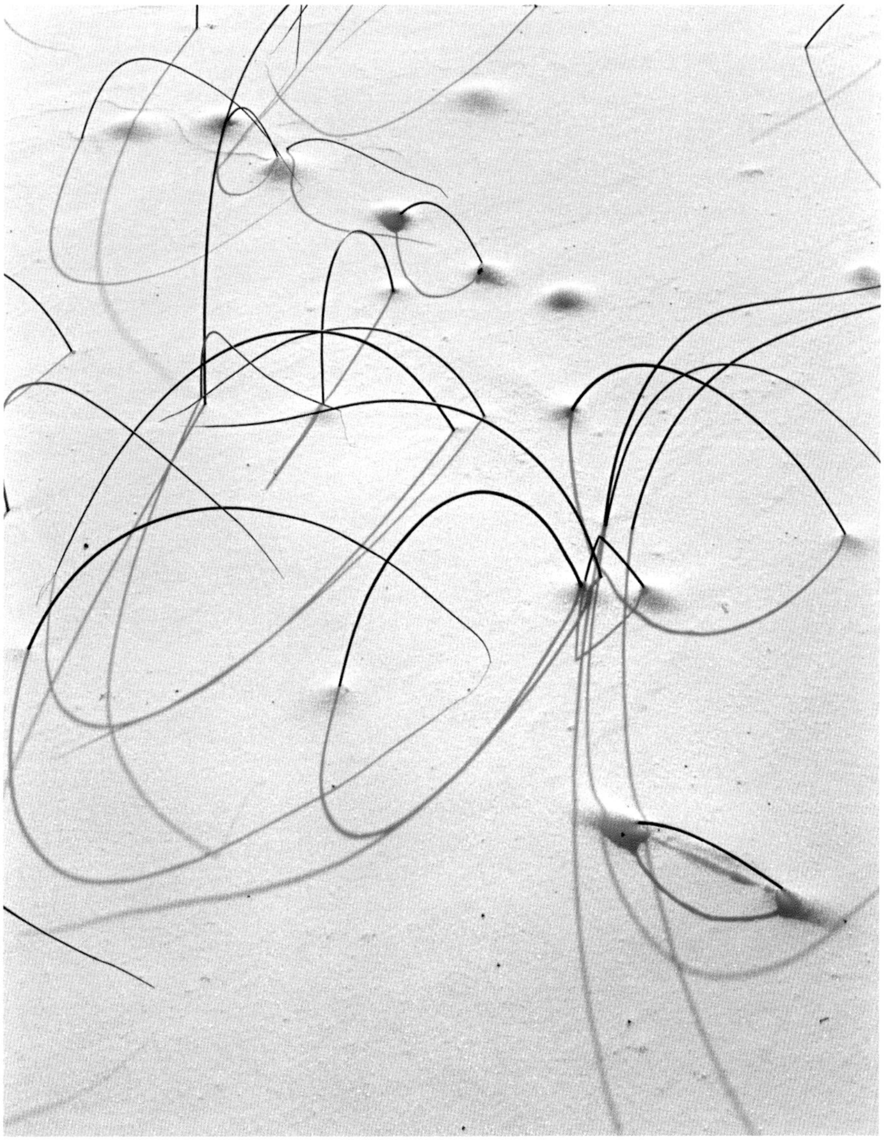

30. Freezing Lake Larson

LEGEND

This we know:

All things are connected, like the blood which unites one family.

Whatever befalls the earth, befalls the sons of the earth.

Man did not weave the web of life, he is but a strand in it.

Whatever he does to the web, he does to himself. [8]

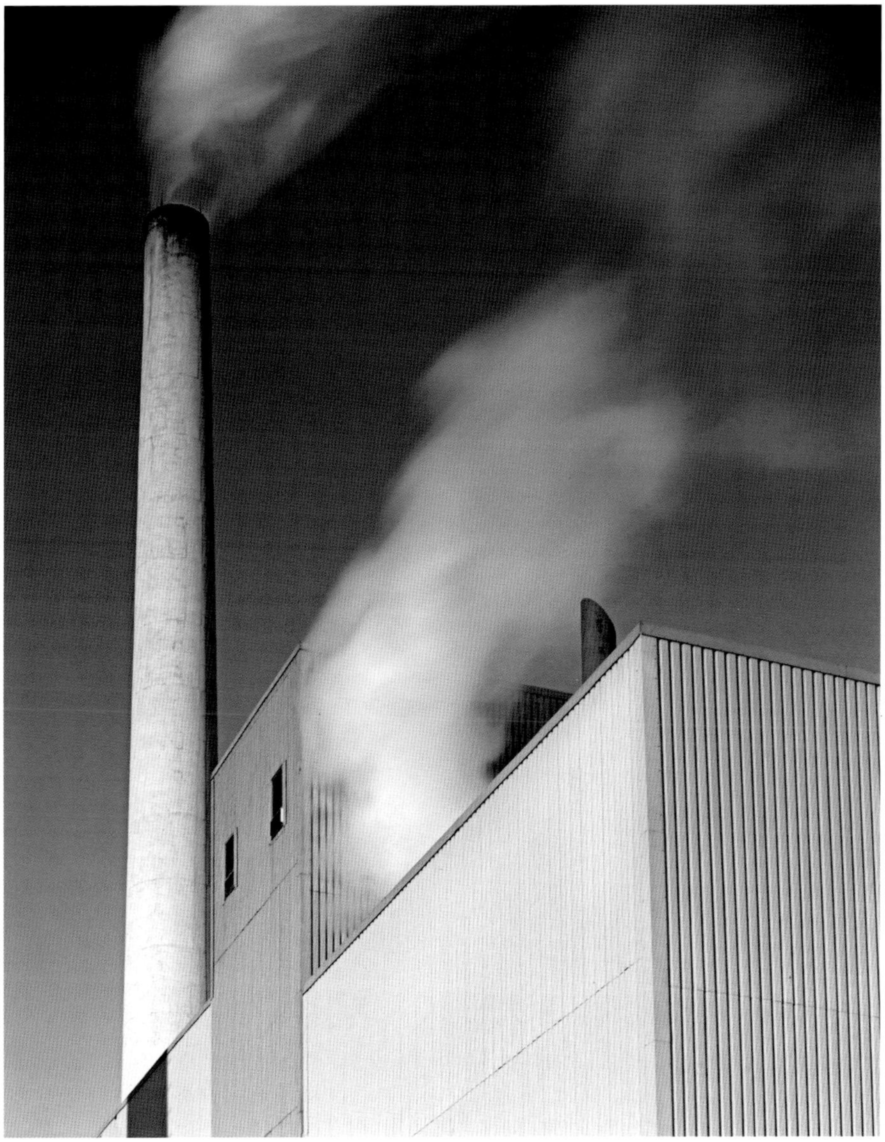

31. Power plant in Moorhead, Minnesota

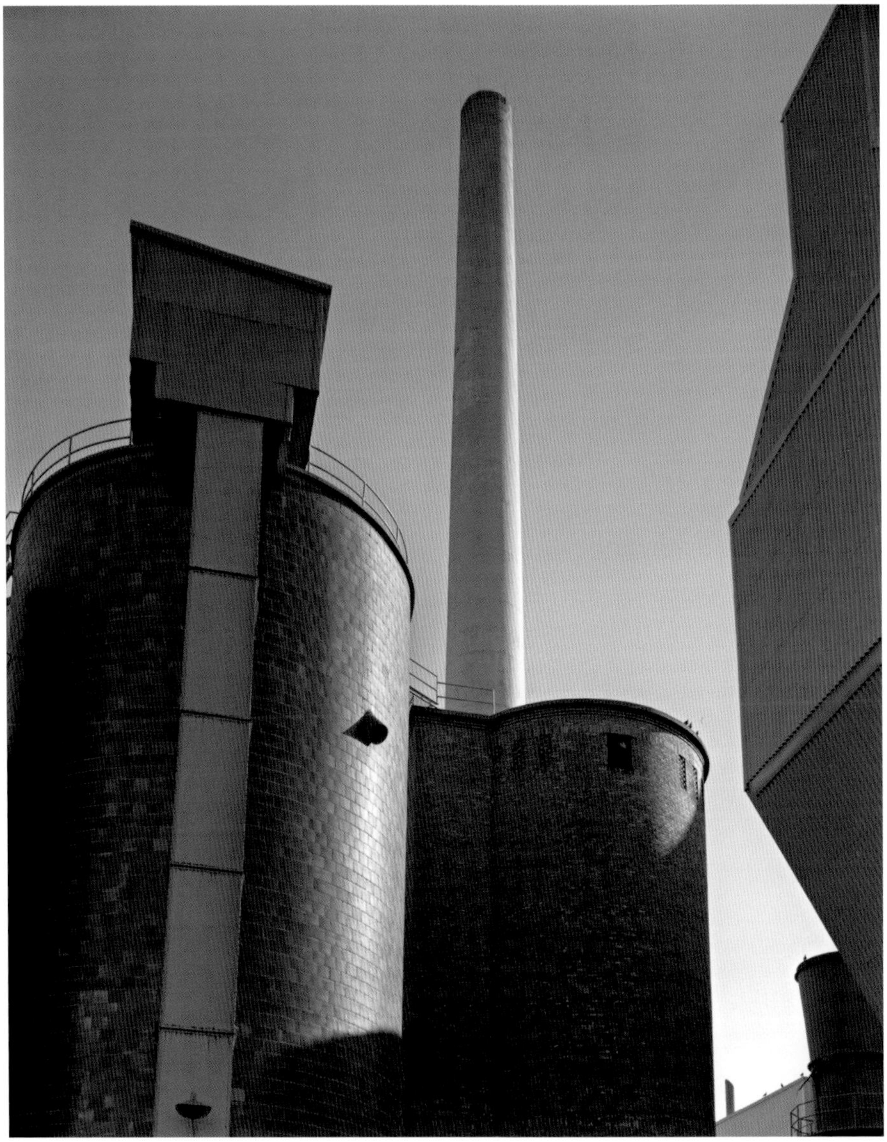

32. Grain silo in western Minnesota

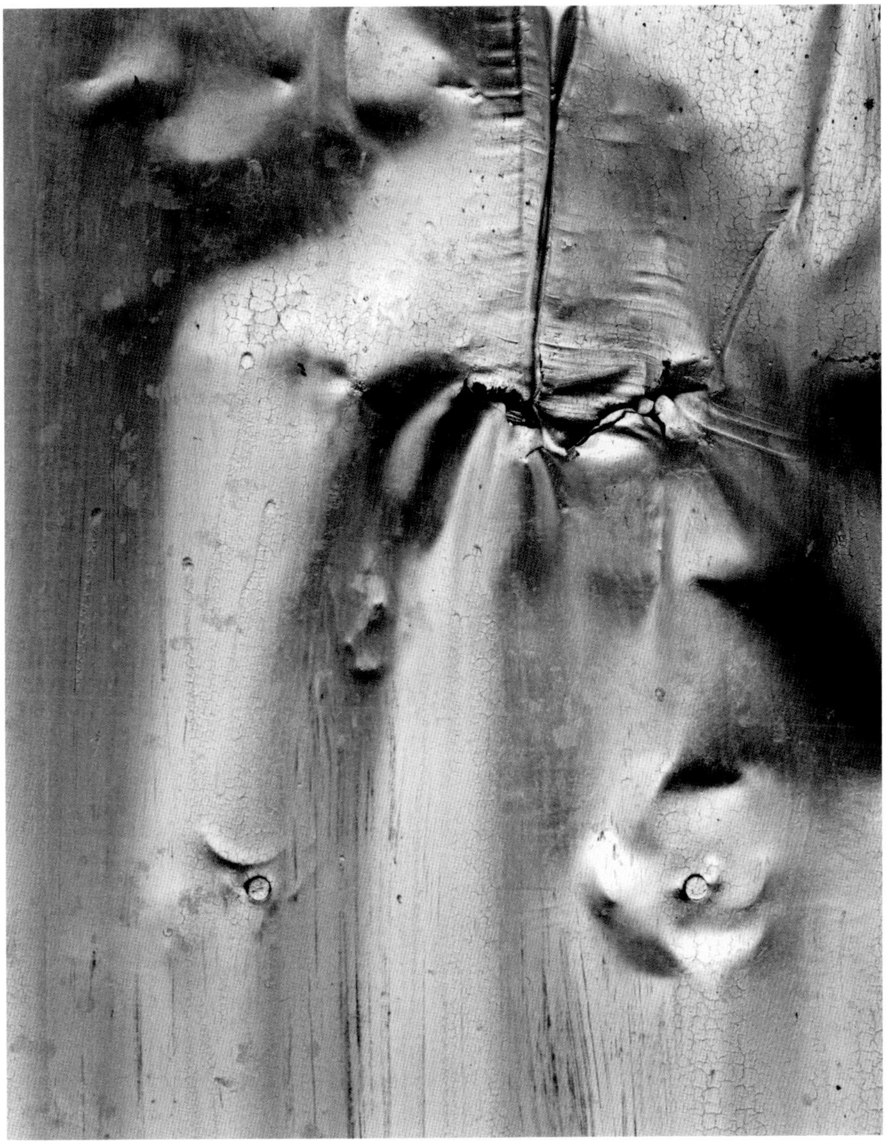

33. Corrugated shroud in Fargo North Dakota

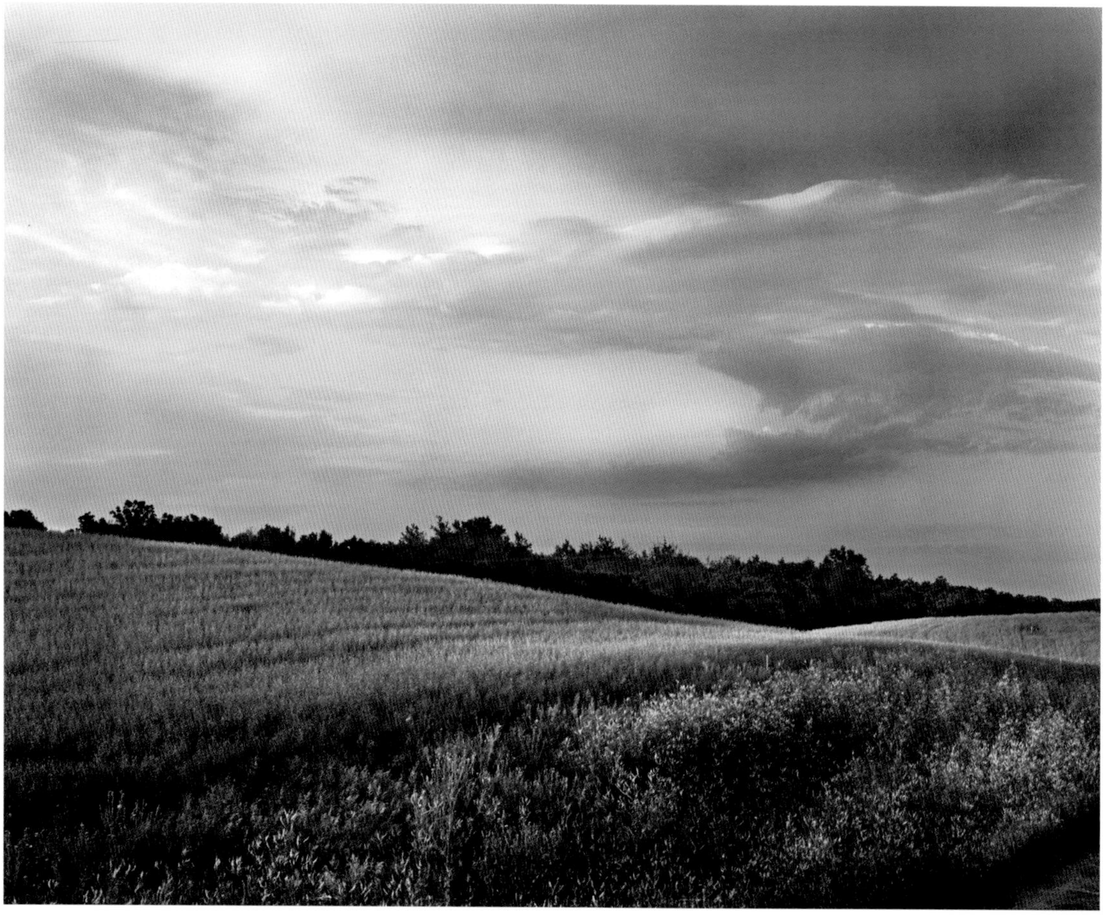

34. Grain fields near Rollog Minnesota

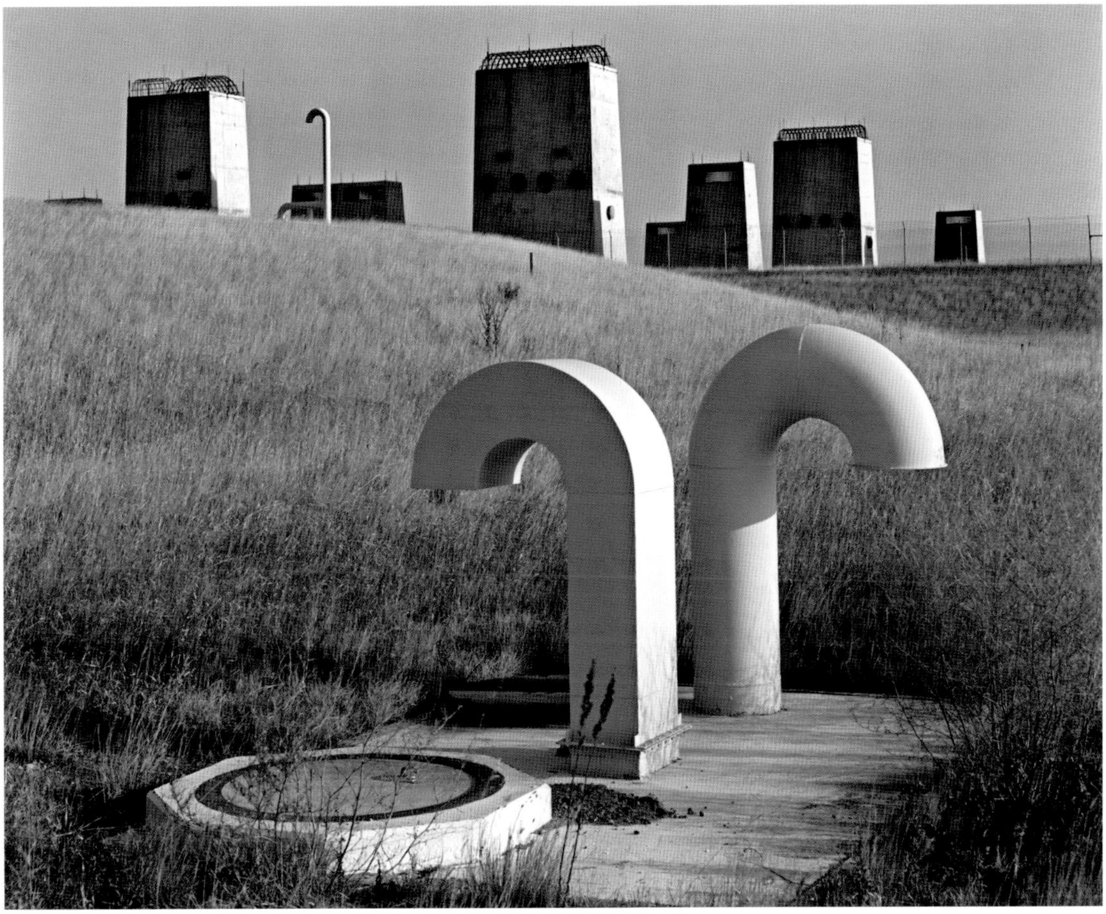

35. Missile silo at Nakoma, North Dakota

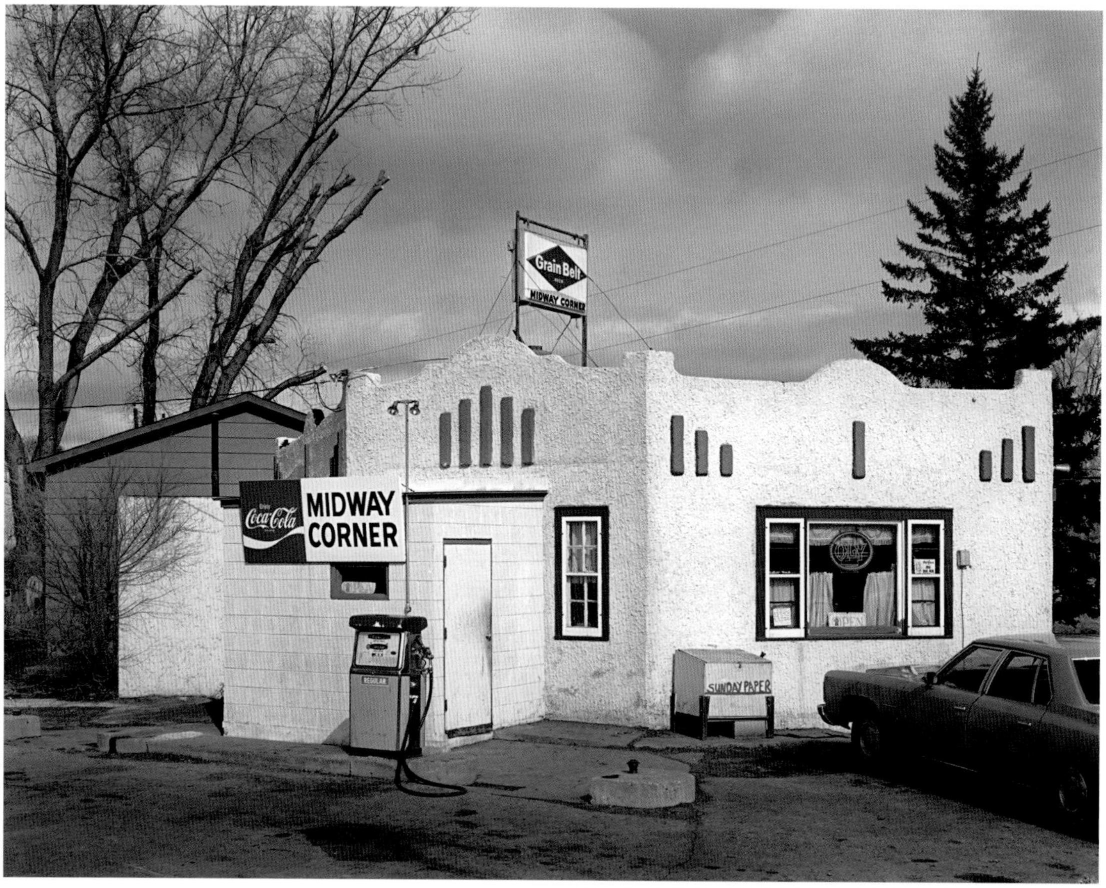

36. Midway in Minnesota

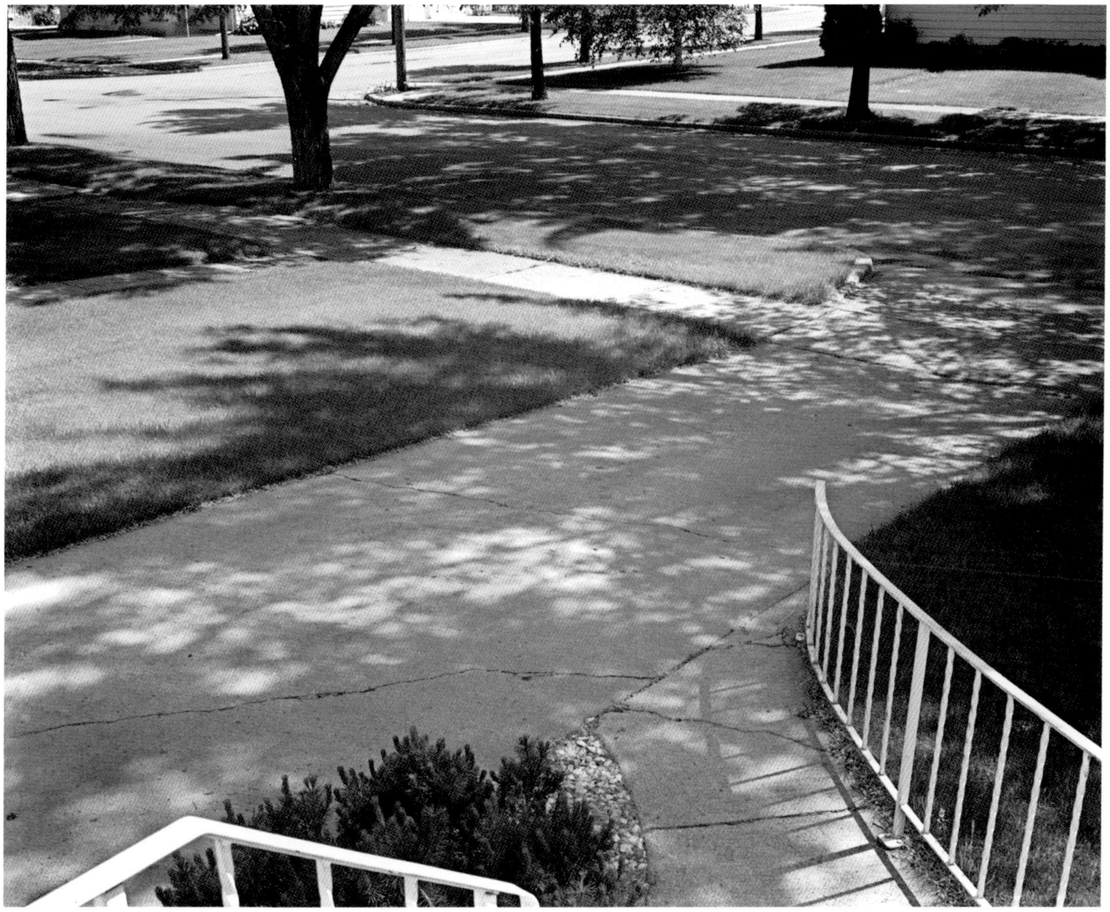

37. South Elm Street Moorhead, Minnesota

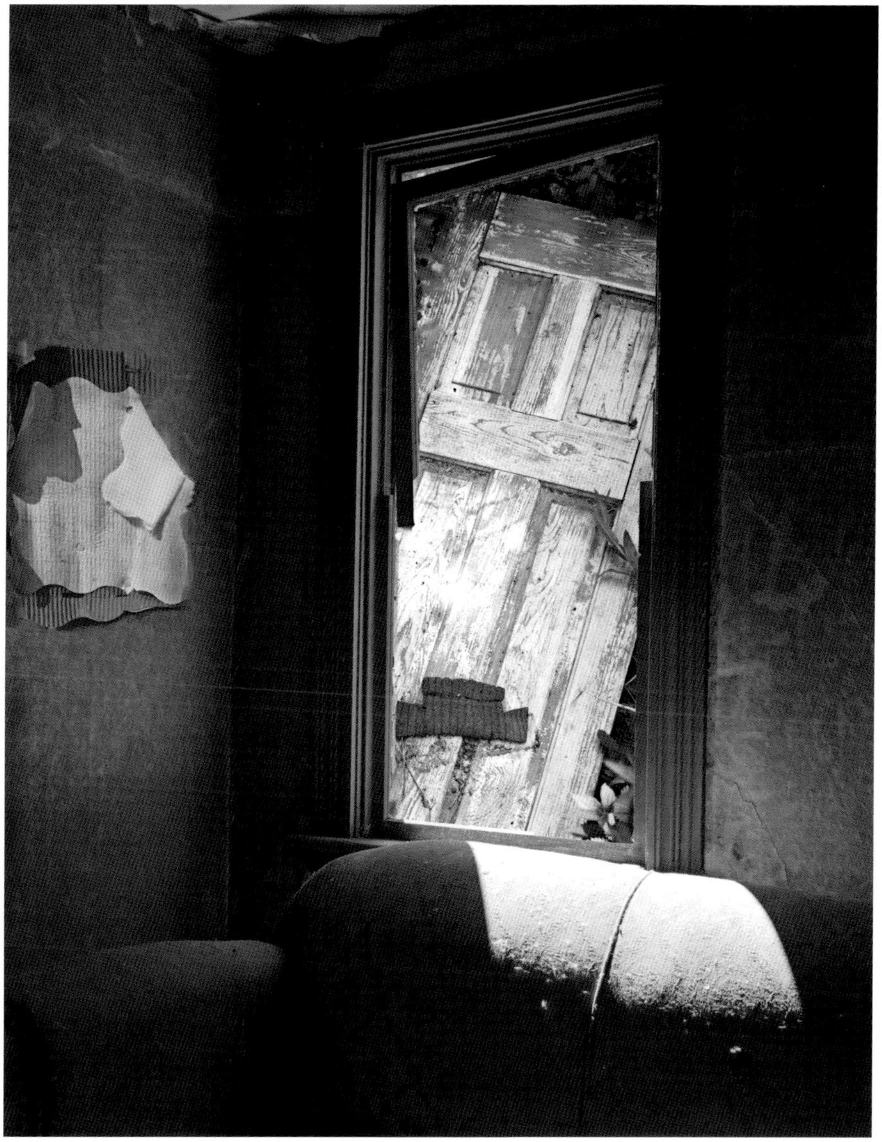

38. Door and window in Abercrombie

In the beginning there was the dream

– Thomas Berry, *The Dream of the Earth*, 1988

After Black Elk

A Review of "Imagining Place"
by Peter Bevan

...a sense sublime
Of something far more deeply interfused,
Whose dwelling is the light of setting suns,
And the round ocean, and the living air,
And the blue sky, and in the mind of man,
A motion and a spirit, that impels
All thinking things, all objects of all thought,
And rolls through all things. [i]

Carll Goodpasture has for some time been convinced of the essential interdependence between human beings and the earth. As an artist, his ambition is for a "return to the primordial community of the universe", exemplified for him, by the perceived connectedness of spiritual philosophy in Native American visionaries like Black Elk. Black Elk was an Oglala Sioux who walked the plains, rivers and forests of the Dakotas over 100 years before Goodpasture began his project.

In a time before European contact and the abiding deprivation of American Indian culture, hunter-gatherers lived in reverence with their environment, investing it with a spiritual ancestry and a living presence. Developing both a kinship and an ecological knowledge, they lived with the land, coming to know every watercourse, every track, rocky outcrop, stand of trees in walking or riding distance. Nothing was profane, spirits were born and dwelt in certain sacred places; everyplace had its spiritual provenance.

Goodpasture yearns for such an integrated heritage in order to regenerate a human perceptual experience of being part of the world, merged within its ecology. With the growing exclusiveness of man from his natural environment he fears an irrevocable evolutionary change in our consciousness disconnected from a sense of place, and ultimately, threatening the very existence of the ecosystem in which we innately belong.

In this ambitious project, his photography is evidence of a search for images which reflect this integration, as he says, "…in a land where Black Elk might have walked". However, this is no simple documentary journey, his photography is purposive; his camera is an "imagining tool" guided to look for signs of spiritual occupation or presence in nature with which he can identify.

However, he proceeds with self-effacement in front of natural phenomena trying instead to connect with currents of universal being of which his "ancestors" were part. Whilst observing the power of nature to continuously transform itself over seasons, he looks for similarities and continuity rather than a "cataloguing" of differences between elemental states ...all things have an animate nature… all things are self-aware of material and spiritual needs of their environment…

The gaze of the photographer is not inquisitive in a pedantic sense, nor acquisitive in the way of a collector. It searches for an experience of the immensity of nature despite being "seen" through the "localised" and partial view of a camera lens. Through this lens he frames exigencies of nature; trees emerging from underground, water flowing over stone, the texture of wind-blown grass, rocks outcropping in swathes of vegetation, changing atmospheric light, the exposure of movement over time, etc., but in the resulting series of photographs he represents the universality of nature and presents pictures of infinity.

Inspired by the spirituality of Native Americans, these photographs have a sense of unity within nature. What he discovers while walking the land are visual and tactile "events" which trigger more generalised reminiscences from a universal store of memories – perhaps a collective memory. These works share for instance, with the photographs of Thomas Joshua Cooper, the recognition of such phenomena in landscape which Cooper refers to as "Unravelling the myth of recollection". [ii] For Goodpasture they embody the "interdependence between human beings and the earth".

It is not surprising that looking at and thinking about this collection of landscape photographs stimulates many literary references, from Wordsworth to Whitman, and perhaps the number is somewhat inflated by my role as a writer! But it may also appropriately mirror the artist's own resource to texts derived from the oral culture of Native Americans. In this review I feel it is important to quote some references at length, not only for their insight, but because they could not be better written and also because they are reminders of things we already know but perhaps, unlike Goodpasture, do rather less than acknowledge.

A generalised but essential interdependence of man and the earth is intimated in "Song of myself" by Walt Whitman:

...A child said, "What is the grass?" fetching it to me with full hands;
How could I answer the child? I do not know what it is any more than he.

I guess it must be the flag of my disposition, out of hopeful green stuff woven.

Or I guess it is the handkerchief of the Lord,
A scented gift and remembrance designedly dropt,
Bearing the owner's name someway in the corners,
That we may see and remark, and say, Whose?

Or I guess the grass is itself a child, the produced babe of the vegetation.

Or I guess it is a uniform hieroglyph,
And it means, Sprouting alike in broad zones and narrow zones,
Growing among black folks as among white,
Kanuck, Tuckahoe, Congressman, Cuff,
I give them the same, I receive them the same.

And now it seems to me the beautiful uncut hair of graves... [iii]

The last stunning line of the quotation embeds our mortality into the very earth from which we arose. The present artist's acknowledgement of a common "ancestral" connection with nature, rather than the exposition of an idiosyncratic personal "vision", enables us as viewers to empathise with his works. His fascination with the continual material transformations in nature (although sometimes metamorphic) are not represented as signs of collapse or disintegration, or with an exaggerated visual language. But rather as a coherent morphology, calmly expressed, perhaps rationalised by the sentiment of belonging - a state of wonder yes, but also of communion with these extraordinary but natural occurrences.

Goodpasture's work triggers in us a sense of the tactility of matter, its weight, consistency and surface, and as Merleau-Ponty reminds us, it is through our bodies that we perceive ourselves in the world; that through the experience and sense of touch our vision is informed. The "knowing gaze" allows the projection of our selves into the "medium" of the world in order to understand our being in it. [iv]

The element of water stimulates contemplative moods universally, and in these photographs Goodpasture particularly relishes the ubiquity and variety of forms of water; the irrepressible flow of clear, cold water, its transformation into heavily blanketed snow, clothing the body of the earth or in Oak tree branching, like a whimsical painter, highlighting with white, certain exposed horizons of natural forms or, with the aid of a breeze, liquefying the reflection of a tree into a "cat o' nine tails" in the surface of a pond (First place to snow along Buffalo River). In Falling water, its movement is "captured" over time and allows us to "see" the generalised form of a "body" of water represented in a viscous flow.

Henry Thoreau brilliantly describes his delight when observing the Spring-thawing sands and clays flowing down the sides of a railway cutting near Walden:

...The material was sand of every degree of fineness and of various rich colors, commonly mixed with a little clay. When the frost comes out in the spring, and even a thawing day in the winter, the sand begins to flow down the slope like lava, sometimes bursting out through

the snow and overflowing it where no sand was to be seen before. Innumerable little streams overlap and interlace one with another, exhibiting a sort of hybrid product, which obeys half the law of currents and half way of vegetation. As it flows it takes the forms of sappy leaves of vines, making heaps of pulpy sprays a foot or more in depth, and resembling, as you look down on them, the lacinated, lobed, and imbricated thalluses of some lichens; or you are reminded of coral, of leopard's paws or bird's feet, of brains or lungs or bowels, and excrements of all kinds…

…Thus it seemed that this one hillside illustrated the principles of all aperations of Nature… [V]

In Goodpasture's pictures there is a similarly visceral and anthropological vision e.g. in the muscular growth of limbs (A way of birch) and in Seven grandfathers mourning, the consequence of a constant wind pressuring the direction of growth of both the trees and grasses, making them lean and bend towards the light, expressing their compulsion for union.

Dragonfly sleeping place reveals a rich awareness of the union of all elements, layered and enmeshing, swathing air forms in the sky, vegetal forms above, on the surface and under the water and the perpetual wind vibrating the myriad stems of grasses.

In other pictures a descending fog enables the air to make itself visible (Morning fog rising at Maplewood). In Feather clouds over Maplewood, high air currents draw clouds around the sky like the swish of a giant hand, and in Praire stones waiting, grasses caress the sacred presences of stones at the behest of the wind.

Stones and trees also stand as markers assertively casting their shadows; they are sentinels of significant places or indicators of pathways (Fallen leaf and Path along Beers Lake). Living, colonising and dying, they continually reclaim their spaces as ageless families (Tree family along Buffalo River).

In "Poeme" 1924, Rilke meditates on the tree as an object of our imaginative perception and describes this as the only way we can fully know the tree, that is, to become it:

If you want to achieve the existence of a tree,
Invest it with inner space, this space
That has its being in you. Surround it with compulsions,
It knows no bounds, and only really becomes a tree
If it takes its place in the heart of your renunciation. [vi]

In the last group of photographs there appears a new subject; the now unsubtle and ominous incursions of man onto the prairies with forms of industrial agriculture; vast mono-cultured fields redefining natural geography, monumental silos, implacable in their clean-cut geometry and aggressive in their assumption of dominance, even more so, when a potential for further aggresion is implicit (Missile silo at Nakoma North Dakota). However, even here in the depiction of a rather brutal technology Goodpasture "softens" its contrast with "raw nature". In images such as Corrugated shroud in Fargo North Dakota, Grain fields near Rollog Minnesota, and Door and window in Abercrombie, these encrustations of man are shown in a process of change as the irrevocable force of nature materially transforms them according to its own aesthetic of beauty. And surely Midway in Minnesota and South Elm Street Moorhead are "markers" and "pathways" on an infinite network of connections almost certainly derived from "ancient" precedents?

I become aware of the incongruity of examining these photographs and writing these thoughts within the dry warm comfort of my home, three thousand miles and more from the land they depict, yet realise that this is a signal of their power. I am transported to these unfamiliar places and walk alongside Goodpasture. The places "imaged" become familiar since they invite my "knowing gaze", triggering inner resources of memory from childhood onwards of the clarity of cold water cascading over granite, of the uncanny silence in deep snow, the sharp echoing crack of thawing ice, the footfall over wind-swept rock, the laboured struggle through dense tufted grasses. There have also been trees whose awe-inspiring solemn presence produced astonishment and induced in me the feeling that here was so different a form of being, but at the least of it, my equal.

This is surely the quality of "imagining" consciousness, being, both curious and compassionate, as essential for a benign relationship with the world?

The artist says "...the natural conditions in which we live constrain our cultural expression". However, through his conjoined inner and outer journeys, Carll Goodpasture emerges from such constraints to make such holistic works, infused as they are with mythology and ecology, and with a prescient desire for unity with our environment. He walks the land with a compulsive energy at-one with the irrepressible energy of nature, and perhaps, his is a journey we should all undertake for our selves and for our collective future?

Glasgow, Scotland
Aug. 2008

i Wordsworth W. From, *Lines compiled near Tintern Abbey*, The English Parnassus: Anthology of longer poems. Oxford University Press. 1921

ii Cooper. T. J. *Between Dark and Dark*. Graeme Murray Gallery, Edinburgh. 1985

iii Whitman W. *Song of myself*, Whitman: Poems. Everyman. 1994

iv Merleau-Ponty M. *Phenomenology of Perception*. Routledge. 2005

v Thoreau H. Spring, in *Walden*. The Portable Thoreau. Ed. Bode C. Penguin Books. 2005

vi Rilke R. M. *Poeme*. 1924

Acknowledgements

The camera work presented here was first encouraged by a friendship and working relationship with the Great Plains photographer and teacher Wayne Gudmundson, who will no doubt appreciate that, even after thirty years of thinking about a picture, it still takes a long time to see.

Sincere appreciation must also go to faculty members of The Glasgow School of Art, especially Ken Mitchell and Peter Bevan for enabling and inspirational guidance to the world of verbalizing about photographs.

For a critical review and discussion of the concept of first peoples sovereignty which underlies this work, I am indebted to Chellis Glendinning of Northern New Mexico.

I must also acknowledge the writings of Thomas Berry, especially his essay The Dream of The Earth, for leading me to a deeper understanding of photography as a kind of practice toward the acquisition of a spiritual dimension to my relationship with the natural environment.

The quotations that address the photographs are attributed to the Native American speakers Eagle Voice, Black Elk, and Chief Seattle. The authenticity of heir words rests on interpretation and reinterpretation through European language and cultural sensibility. Although the quoted passages may be inauthentic and thus works of fiction, they represent an indigenous contribution to the evolving myth of the earth as an animate and interconnected whole. The principal source consulted was John G. Neihardt's Black Elk Speaks, a poetic story of Oglala Sioux spiritual belief.

I owe a special note of thanks to the University of Nebraska Press for having kindly granted permission to quote at length from Black Elk Speaks.

Finally, and most deservedly, I am indebted to my life partner, Gro Heining, for support and encouragement in bringing the work to its present completed form.

AMERICAN INDIAN QUOTATION SOURCES

1. As quoted by John G. Neihardt in *When The Tree Flowered*, University of Nebraska Press, 1970, p. 23.
2. John G. Neihardt, *Black Elk Speaks: Being the life Story of a Holy Man of the Oglala Sioux as told through John G. Neihardt*, University of Nebraska Press, 1979, pp. 1 & 35.
3. ibid. p. 85.
4. ibid. pp. 41 & 42.
5. From an ancient traditional Lakota prayer addressed to The Great Spirit, as recited in part by Black Elk in the telling of his vision in *Black Elk Speaks* and as recorded by Edward S. Curtis in *The North American Indian*, Northwestern University Library, 2003, http://digital.library.northwestern.edu/curtis/.
6. Neihardt, op.cit. pp. 42, 43, & 242.
7. Joseph Epes Brown, The Sacred Pipe, University of Oklahoma Press, 1953. pp. 46 & 47.
8. Attributed to Chief Seattle in *How Can One Sell The Air?: Chief Seattle's Vision*. The Book Publishing Company, 1992.

Edition of one thousand copies published by
Imago ans, Ing. Hoelsv. 47, N-1346 Gjettum, Norway
www.goodpasture.ritardando.net

Text Carll Goodpasture and Peter Bevan

ISBN 978-82-998015-0-8

Design and composition / Imago ans

Prepress and printing/ Pettit Network Inc., Afton, Minnesota
Printed in China

Typeface/ Copperplate and Adobe Garamond

Inks/ Black + Pantone Warm Gray + gloss spot varnish on photographs

Paper/ Gold East 157 gsm matt art